Rowel Friers was born in Belfast in 1920 and was educated at Park Parade Intermediate School. After leaving school at the age of fifteen, he first served as an apprentice lithographer, and then went on to study at the Belfast College of Art. In 1953 the Council for the Encouragement of Music and the Arts hosted his first exhibition of paintings, drawings and cartoons. His work has appeared in numerous newspapers and journals, including the *Belfast Telegraph*, *Irish Times*, *Ulster News Letter*, *Daily Express*, *London Opinion*, *Dublin Opinion*, *Punch* and *Radio Times*. In addition to designing sets for the Lyric Theatre and Northern Ireland Opera, he has worked for and appeared in numerous programmes for the BBC and Ulster Television. He has published nine collections of cartoons, including best-sellers *Riotous Living* and *Pig in the Parlour*, and he has also illustrated more than thirty books. Currently president of the Royal Ulster Academy of Arts, he has exhibited there and at the Royal Hibernian Academy in Dublin. In 1977 he was awarded an MBE for contributions to journalism and art. He lives in Holywood, County Down, and is married with three children.

D1543913

Rowel Fr

Drawn *from* Life

AN AUTOBIOGRAPHY

U.S. DISTRIBUTOR
DUFOUR EDITIONS
CHESTER SPRINGS,
PA 19425-0007
(610) 458-5005

THE
BLACKSTAFF
PRESS

BELFAST

The publishers would like to thank the Deputy Keeper of the Records of the Public Record Office of Northern Ireland for permission to reproduce the photographs on pages 98 and 99 (ref. CAB 3A and CAB 68).

First published in 1994 by
The Blackstaff Press Limited
3 Galway Park, Dundonald, Belfast BT16 0AN, Northern Ireland
with the assistance of
The Arts Council of Northern Ireland
© Rowel Friers, 1994
All rights reserved

Typeset by Paragon Typesetters, Queensferry, Clwyd

Printed in Northern Ireland by
W. & G. Baird Limited

A CIP catalogue record for this book
is available from the British Library

ISBN 0-85640-539-6

CONTENTS

PREFACE

I put it down to being incapable of keeping my mouth shut. Reminiscing overmuch with friends is fatal; quite suddenly they get wildly enthusiastic about writing an autobiography – that is to say, they get enthusiastic about *you* writing one. And once the idea has taken hold, you become the target for breathless enquiries: 'Have you started it yet?'; 'How much have you written?'; 'You must write about...', et cetera, et cetera. The fever mysteriously spreads to people you barely know and 'How is it coming on?' becomes a catch phrase. So, encouraged by Yvonne and the family and some friends, who all worked as hard as I did, the challenge was taken up.

Drawn from Life would never have been written without the help of those friends. Eileen Orr was able to translate my hieroglyphics into readable type and her comments encouraged me to keep going. Then Iza Fowweather (who drove her mother to write *Other Days Around Me* and *Roses and Rainbows*, and her late husband Arthur to pen *One Small Head* and *Up Down*) – not only did she spur me on but she actually hammered the keys and worked unsparingly correlating the chapters; and her sister Joan, who was good enough to cast a critical eye thereon. Norma Rutherford, who did the final wordprocessing, made the whole presentation a thing to be proud of. One man stands alone, journalist and art collector Michael Drake, who cast a professional eye on the manuscript and whose co-operation was invaluable.

Rowel Friers
Holywood
August 1994

For Yvonne, Vivien,
Jeremy and Timothy

1

THE EARLY YEARS

IT WAS ONE OF THOSE NIGHTS which seem to be exclusively Irish. The month of October had not started too well and was apparently making no hopeful promises. The rain did not fall, but instead it drifted, fine and wet, gossamer-like, breaking on the face like a cold perspiration. Because of the rain, the darkness was intense. Paradoxically, despite the blackness, the cobbles in the entry glinted every now and then, conjuring up an eerie light from some mysterious source. Here and there a puddle fitfully blinked its presence.

The mother's breathing was keeping pace with the rapid movement of her feet as she fought against her fear and the night. The child was clutched firmly to her breast, becoming part of herself; to remove him would have taken surgery. She kept moaning to herself as she ran. 'My baby. Oh, my poor baby.' Hope replaced terror as she neared the end of this, her tenth or twelfth long dark Belfast entry. I'm home now, she thought, hugging the child even closer. She raced towards the end and suddenly, there he was, towering over her, blocking her path, black and menacing, his night helmet rain-haloed by a street lamp.

'And where do you think you're going?'

His voice was gruff and, to her, bore a threatening note. Panic took control as she thought of the baby in her arms.

'Oh, my child, my child,' she panted, pressing her offspring near to asphyxiation.

'What's wrong with the baby?' he asked, with obvious concern in his voice.

'Nothing,' she replied, 'we just need to get home.'

Suddenly remembering his duty, he became a policeman once more. 'And what are you doing out after curfew?' he demanded.

'I was at my sister-in-law's and forgot the time, constable,' she muttered apologetically.

Recognising the voice, the policeman's tone changed. 'Ach, it's you, Mrs Friers, What the hell's got into you? You know the dangers after curfew time.' He knew her well enough not to waste time preaching to the unreceptive. 'Come on an' I'll see you the rest of the way.'

That was in the twenties. The days of Michael Collins, de Valera, James Craig, Carson, and so on, 'No surrender', 'Not an inch', 'British out', 'Ireland for the Irish' and all the other partisan slogans that then abounded, when Catholic and Protestant roared defiance and indulged in the national sport of killing each other. Orange and Green, Black and Tan, were the colours fashion decreed; curfew and police tenders; days when men became martyrs and women became widows. Now, in the senseless nineties, has anything changed?

The opening paragraphs of this autobiography are a reconstruction of a dramatic event. The author, whilst having a reasonably vivid memory of past events, could not possibly have recalled that particular night, as he (being the babe in arms) was most likely asleep at the time. But the tale was much repeated throughout the author's early years and thus seemed destined to open this, his story.

My father hailed from Monaghan and was a cashier in the Irish Distillery at Connswater in east Belfast. Mother was of country stock and was born in the Black Mountain region of Belfast. When they were first married they settled in the Bloomfield area, before moving to a house at the bottom of the Ravenhill Road in the Lagan Village. Here I was born in 1920 in a tall Victorian building, housing on the bottom floor a tobacco and confectionery business that my mother ran. The house was sandwiched between another shop and a public house. A narrow cobbled alleyway, McMullan's Lane, cut alongside the bar, separating this commercial trio from a dark, sombre, flat-roofed edifice – the Boyd Endowment Public Elementary School, our local fount of learning. This foursome of red-brick giants towered over the whitewashed cottages on the opposite side of the square-setted and tram-lined road, at the heart of Lagan Village.

Our family consisted of three boys and three girls: Bill, the eldest, Cambridge, a couple of years younger, Edna, Ian, Helen and, as an after-thought, rather later than safety permits, I was born. Helen had died at the tender age of six, during the years of the First World War, victim of a hideous influenza epidemic that had swept the country. I was born five years later. Edna, who was very dark and beautiful, worked in Norman Brands (later Brands and Normans) department store with Cambridge. She was extremely popular and a real live wire, the combination of which may have contributed to her sudden death at the age

of eighteen. Cambridge used to tell me: 'One day she washed her hair and went straight out on a pillion ride with a boyfriend, and afterwards she caught a dreadful fever.' At that time the sisters shared a bed, and Cambridge told me how Edna had developed a raging temperature that night and, to her sister's alarm, she had said she was going to die. The local doctor was summoned, but did not arrive until daybreak, when sadly all he could do was pronounce Edna dead. After this tragedy Edna's name could never be mentioned in Mother's presence, that hideously cruel blow having left an irreparable scar on her mind. She could never bear to be reminded of the nightmare that had robbed her of a favourite child. Cambridge was convinced that Edna must have had a dormant lung infection to succumb so rapidly. In the twenties pneumonia took many lives, and double pneumonia was an even deadlier roulette.

Mother was small, just over five feet, slim and active, or, more correctly, super-active. Fast and positive in everything she did, Mother could have been a really successful career woman had she not met Dad and 'looked for a soft seat!' This, her own expression, she used as a warning to her sons against women with designs on them. She had a good complexion and Titian hair like Cambridge, the only differences being length and style. Cambridge wore a short bob, whereas Mother always had her hair brushed neatly back, with a plaited bun at the nape of her neck. When she undid her tresses, her hair reached down past her waistline. From time to time she suffered from migraines and it would be no exaggeration to say we suffered from them as much or more. She would retire to bed with a wet towel on her head and moan theatrically. The moans would be interspersed with 'Oh, I'm dying', or 'Oh, I'm bad', all with enough volume to give the listeners a headache. We all knew she liked attention and much of her suffering verged on a dramatic ploy to engage that attention. This is no cruel cynicism, because often in the middle of a dying routine, some friend would ring her to ask her out and the recovery could be instant.

Having been born up around the Black Mountain, my mother had many country turns of phrase. With her, people could be 'sluthers' or 'wee oul' snules' or 'glypes' or 'pochles'. I remember being at a cousin's wedding when a somewhat pompous cleric was making a lengthy speech, and Mother whispering sideways: 'That's a sore mouth! He's full of himself.' She feared no one and I remember a story told to me by

My mother Helen and myself, c. 1927

an aunt that illustrated this fearlessness. During the Troubles of the 1920s, the story went, Mother was informed by a customer that two men were in the pub next door holding guns on Mr and Mrs Doran with intent to kill. Out she dashed, eyes blazing, and through the swing doors into the bar. Two local hard men had indeed guns to hand and were threatening our Catholic neighbours. The gunslingers stole a rapid and nervous glance at the door, expecting the RUC, no doubt, and not Mrs Friers. She knew them both and immediately launched her attack.

'What do you two Johnnies think you're doing here? How dare you come in with those stupid things in your hands? These people are your friends and you know it. How often have you had free drinks from them, and how often drinks on tick? You should be ashamed of yourselves. Apologise to Mr and Mrs Doran, put those things away, and get out of here.'

Two thunderstruck tough guys apologised shamefacedly, and sidled out into the night. Somehow I cannot imagine that such initiative would be quite so effective in today's climate.

I remember my Uncle Tom, a most pompous and overbearing Englishman, finding himself losing an argument to Mother, and crying in exasperation: 'Dammit, Nellie, you're nothing but a cheeky little puppy dog biting at the heels of a thoroughbred horse.' The analogy was good but somewhat ludicrous when you looked at Uncle Tom's corpulence and at the same time tried to imagine the sleekness of a thoroughbred.

My father, so it seemed, was not made of the same stern stuff as his wife. I was told by Mother of an incident during the Troubles which graphically emphasised their contrasting personalities. Apparently, when discussing the turbulent situation, a question arose as to how they imagined they would react if faced by a gunman. Father was categorical about how he would handle such a problem. He reasoned that, in the unlikely possibility of such a confrontation, he would face up to the gunman calmly and reason with him. No need for panic. When you yourself have no strong political opinions, other people can always be reasoned with. That was his firm conviction.

One evening, about three weeks later, Father had not returned from work at the usual time. Mother was becoming concerned. She knew he was not working overtime so she suspected the worst. The household was tense until the breadwinner eventually strode in with great dignity, a little too much dignity, in fact, a telltale sign of a man having had a drop too much. His bowler hat was at a jaunty angle and his walking stick, taking most of his weight, had become his third and most stable leg.

'Where have you been to this hour?' A question posed that required no answer. 'What on earth happened to you?' she added.

Peering at Mother with sad eyes, as wide as he could get them and adjusting focus, he announced, in a matter-of-fact way, that he had been held up.

'Held up? How?' asked Mother, suspecting he had met some cronies on the way home.

'At the office,' said he, 'with a gun – a man with a gun.'

'With a gun? What did you do?' Mother gasped.

'I gave him the money,' he replied, shrugging his shoulders non-chalantly.

Trying to contain her amusement, Mother reminded him of how he had proposed to react under such circumstances.

His reply was logical and disarming. 'Helen,' he said, 'I was counting

'A minute, please! I must insist on your signing some sort of receipt.'

the money when this young man burst into the office and demanded I hand over the lot.'

'Didn't you talk to him? Didn't you reason him out of it?' enquired Mother, with Father's theory still in mind and no doubt with a sly smile on her face.

'I couldn't talk. My mouth went dry. I just pushed all the money towards him.'

'Why on earth didn't you do what you said you would do in the circumstances?' she demanded.

'The time seemed to last for ever. The young fellow was terrified, the revolver in his hand was shaking at the rate of his pulse. His nerves were out of control and his finger was on the trigger. The money wasn't mine, I had nothing to lose but my life, the distillery could afford to lose the cash and not miss it, but I could not afford the heroics.'

In contrast to Mother, my father was a very relaxed, bookish man. Edna's death was a major contributory factor to the stroke that ended his life in 1926. Though he lived for only six years of my life, his personality was so strong that he might have died but a few months ago . . .

The huge toecap of the boot shone like a black mirror. I could almost see myself in it, and when I reached forward with a tiny hand, my fingertips reflected back like balloons on tapering pink stalks. I studied the boot carefully, wondering at its size; then moving over on my haunches, I placed my sandalled foot beside this object of interest. The comparison was such that I could only gasp. Should the giant wish, I thought, he could just trample me flat like a cat run over by a charabanc. A grey hand-knitted sock, having detached itself from a suspender, corrugated itself heavily over the ankle of the boot. A small white area of skin lay exposed between sock and trouser end. My eyes travelled up the giant's leg, with its acres of tweed that seemed to stretch for ever. A large hand, pink and plump, lay palm upward on the great thigh from where a discarded newspaper had fallen untidily over the other leg. Higher still my childish eyes noted the well-filled waistcoat bedecked with a heavy gold watch chain that looped from pocket to pocket, with the added adornment of a large jade fob mounted in gold. The waistcoat rose and fell slowly, in perfect rhythm with the gentle snore issuing from the giant. I wondered why he was sleeping. Had he been reading a bedtime story, and if so, why did he still have his hat on? Was he too tired to

take it off? The bowler rested rakishly and precariously on the back of his bald head. A pair of gold-rimmed reading glasses angled dangerously on the end of his nose and an expression of bliss enveloped the good-natured rosy face. Obviously it was bedtime, so the tiny adoring observer proceeded to undo the laces of his father's boots.

'Don't do that, son' – my mother's voice was sharp – 'if your father wakens, he'll trip.'

I stopped on command, as we always did when our mother spoke. On my hands and knees I scurried across to the feet of the beautiful and very kind giant who was my sister Edna. I was just going on four, and she was sixteen. I lived in a land of giants and one of my favourite occupations was loosening their laces. Sometimes when the giants wished to be entertained, they would get me to do my special trick. This was a death-defying act, when they lifted me to a shelf above the kitchen door, from which I hung by my tummy – no hands. This trick was to prove useful training for later years when a bar counter came within sight.

My earliest Christmas recollection is very mixed. I was put to bed earlier than usual that night and was told there would be something special for me if I was a good boy and went to sleep. It was 'the very next day many, many years before', I was informed, 'that the baby Jesus was born, and He, as we all knew, wasn't quite as lucky as some where beds were concerned. However, He had plenty of visitors who brought Him gifts.' Now, although Jesus did have visitors, He did not have the same one who was to come on this night. A good reason for this over-sight was that the same person did not exist that far back. The gentleman in question was fat and merry and had red clothes with a matching face. His hat and suit were trimmed with white fur and he had a long white beard and colour-matched bushy eyebrows. He rode through the sky on a sleigh pulled by reindeer, and the sleigh was laden to capacity with toys. Should a boy or girl be bad and not go to sleep, then White Beard would pass by and not fill the stocking which hung at the end of the bed.

I was tucked in snugly, and again told to be good, the lights were put out and I was left with my thoughts. My one great desire was to act on the advice given and get to sleep fast. However, darkness and an over-active imagination were not conducive to the slumber I desperately sought. The room was very dark, with only a tiny slot of light where the door had been left slightly ajar. A yellowish glow filtered up from the bottom landing. Supposing Wee Nick gets here first? Would he get

ROWEL FRIERS

in the bed and catch me, as was his wont with others? 'You never know he's there until he grabs you', I had been told. Wee Nick was always on the prowl, looking for small boys and girls. How he dealt with them was never revealed, but in my small mind their fate just had to be gruesome.

Wee Nick was the creation of my older brothers. In bed at nights they would say in tiny, high-pitched voices, 'Here's Wee Nick' and 'I'm Wee Nick comin' till get ye.' Although I could never quite put a face to the voice, my mental picture was of an ever-so-tiny, black, hairy man. The eyes, I imagined, were red and his teeth yellow and sharp, and his height no more than six or seven inches. There were times when the fabrications of Wee Nick had me hopping out of bed in terror to seek sanctuary between my parents. This was possibly not that popular with them, but incredibly comforting to me.

On top of one menace, I now had another – this Santa Claus, a gigantic red and white ghost. I must find sleep before either or both got near me. Eventually, Morpheus beat them to the bedpost and the tortured mind became as the room, with darkness taking over.

Next morning I woke early. Anticipation at fever pitch, I reached for the bulging stocking. A small wind-up orange racing car fell out as I upended the stocking's contents onto the floor. My face dropped as sweets and bars of chocolate followed, plus a handful of cinders. It was explained to me later that the cinders were from Santa's clothes, that had accumulated during his chimney trip. This was acceptable enough, but why did the oul' goat leave me confectionery when there was a shopful downstairs? Who could have believed in a nutcase like

Complaints

"Still four weeks to Christmas and already your Santa has no hearty laugh, is showing signs of disinterest, traces of irritability, and has had a complete loss of characterisation."

that? For some years afterwards the oul' fool kept delivering much the same thing. Occasionally, he would ring the changes from ordinary milk chocolate to fruit and nut. Though I always enjoyed the atmosphere and excitement created at Christmas I am afraid, where I was concerned, White Beard contributed little more than frustration.

Those days, when I was the centre of the grown-ups' attention, may well have been my happiest. No responsibilities – just the big folks' source of amusement. With help, I could nearly stand on my head, and like the rest of my family, I could draw. My very favourite hiding place was behind the settee where, in secluded security, I would rapidly sketch the likenesses of unsuspecting visitors. These lightning drawings would be passed out for a sister or a brother to make the presentation. 'Look what Baby can do,' they would say, and I would shake baby hands in frantic excitement at the impression I was creating. This is how egos are born. Baby, as I was to be called until about the age of fifteen, was always very excitable. I had an uncontrollable habit, when enthusiastic, of leaping up and down and shaking my hands wildly. A great surge of electric current seemed to run through my whole being, then off I would go like a jumping jack. To this day I can feel that excitement mount within me but the dancing is no more, partly because I am convinced it would not be entirely acceptable in social circles. Those dancing sessions occurred most regularly when my father was about to take me out for a walk. Mother would have the greatest difficulty in buttoning my coat, with me on the bounce as I spied my dad reaching for a walking stick – like a dog when it sees the lead, the only difference being that the dog shakes its tail, whereas I shook my hands.

It was a strange word, one I had heard on a few occasions before. As a word it was intriguing, mysterious, not a word that sounded English. It had a sharp ring to it and it seemed to have quite some impact when used. On a particular occasion when I heard it, I resolved to know what it meant. I was at that stage in my life when I liked new words, particularly as I had now overcome the infant stage of expressing myself. Babyhood had gone for ever. I was a big boy now. This word would be a breakthrough. It was a big boy's word. Oh, how wrong I was, what a misapprehension I was under.

At my still-tender age you learned most things at home. All you ever had to do was ask. Turning the strange word round in my mind, I walked purposefully towards the shop, in at the front door, past the counters, through to the kitchen where a ring of visitors sat, in communion, round the shining range. They were aunts and uncles and a couple of neighbours all in their Sunday best, looking very sedate and sipping tea and eating sandwiches. They must have been at somebody's funeral for it was not a Sunday. Determined to find the secret of the word, I marched straight to centre stage and turned my back to the fire. They chatted quietly, almost reverently, with much head-nodding, all ignoring the small knowledge-seeking plump figure. Then I launched it at them with full theatrical projection – FUCK!

Without any doubt that word did mean something. A spoon was dropped, sounding like a girder on the tiled floor. A clatter of cups, gasps of surprise, then a deathly silence. Horrified eyes glared at me as though I had just materialised from hell. Then something hit me on the side of the head, stars cavorted merrily before my eyes, my ear was twisted violently and painfully. Suddenly I was in my bedroom, quite possibly breaking the sound barrier *en route*.

2

GROWING UP IN LAGAN VILLAGE

THE WALKS WITH MY FATHER were magical journeys, mostly along the Albertbridge Road, which ran at right angles to the Ravenhill Road, about four hundred yards from our house. Often my father would stop at Twomey's, a tiny greengrocer's shop that displayed much of its wares in a patchwork of colour on stalls outside the premises. Here he would buy some fruit and, as often as not, present his wide-eyed son with a rosy peach or some equally delectable morsel. Sometimes the walk would be over the Albert Bridge itself, towards the cattle pens at Maysfield. The child's mind wondered what May was like and why she called this square-setted iron-railed area a field. The electricity station directly opposite the pens, on the corner of the Sand Quay (now the Laganbank Road), towered skywards, emanating Victorian melancholy. Its heaviness and depressiveness would have allowed it to fit well into Red Square in Moscow and not look out of place architecturally. On an autumn evening, steam would rise from the tightly crowded pens, creating a bluish fog that curled around in the yellow lamplight of the bovine prison. To me, the cattle looked sad; my father said they were waiting for the trains to take them away. Where were they going? I was not told, but they gave no obvious impression that it was going to be a holiday. Every now and then a head would be thrust heavenwards, and with white eyeballs rolling, an animal would give full vent to its feelings in a long hollow moan. This made me unhappy and a gentle pull on my father's cuff was a sufficient cue for us to move back across the bridge. The lamps on the parapet, writhingly ornamental, cast their yellow gaslight on the black Lagan below. Their reflections wriggled on the rhythmical flowing river like golden serpents. Years later, a war, blacker than the Lagan that night, was to be waged against

Germany and its allies, and in that war human beings were to be treated like the cattle whose lives I had so instinctively feared for.

About twice weekly the Lagan Village was transformed into a Wild West setting when the big cattle drive thundered down the Ravenhill Road, past our shop. Terrified animals huddled together in fear of the traffic, their hooves slithering on the square sets and shining tramlines. The cowboys who drove the cattle towards the city and to their pens were not mounted men in stetsons wearing fancy riding boots, just scruffy youths with bespattered moleskin trousers and pudding-bowl haircuts. The trail boss was a grizzled veteran with an embossed red-leather face, a much-stained raincoat, trousers tied with string, a duncher cap pulled well down to the bridge of his nose and a clay pipe held tight in what remained of yellow teeth. He carried a heavy stick that he bounced off the rumps of his steers as and when he thought it necessary. Naturally enough, trail bosses changed, but the mould had little variation.

There were days when a really big drive would cause utter chaos, days when traffic would come to a standstill, trams clanging their bells, motorists honking their horns and cursing as their cars rocked under the impact of panicking animals – all united to create a cacophony of sound that was sheer bedlam. I was to watch this excitement from the shelter of our closed shop door. The wild-eyed bovine stampede was not something easily faced by a small boy. On one occasion, when the door was inadvertently left open, a half-crazed steer rushed into the shop. Penned in by two counters and pursued by a loud-mouthed gesticulating youth, the desperate animal charged around in small circles, butting and kicking in an attempt to escape its drover. Bottles flew in all directions, exploding on the tiled floor and spraying Barker and Dobson's and Clarnico's in all directions. The floor was wall-to-wall in finest confectionery and broken glass.

On our outings to the Albertbridge Road my excitement would reach fever pitch. Past Hugh Gemmell's black and white pudding shop we went, a shop noted not only for puddings but also for the proprietor's unique advertising talents. He had poetry in his soul and shared his gift with the rest of the world at large by writing odes to his undoubted prowess as a pudding manufacturer. These he displayed on large posters on his shop front. They were churned out almost as constantly as his products. I gathered that the quality of his puddings was never questioned, but his verse was not always quite so easily digested.

The Albertbridge Road was a busy shopping area and the windows of the many different stores presented great visual adventures to a young observer. Two shops I was to get to know well were the Maypole and Dunlop's: the Maypole, next door to Dunlop's, was all green, with its name in gold paint; Dunlop's was dark red with its name also in gold. Both shops faced Mount Street and it was when I was about seven, after my father's death, that I started going to Dunlop's for 'a pound and a half of Danish butter and a pound of Red Label tea'. Why I was unable to get these products in my own territory remained a mystery. Through the years I beat a track from the Ravenhill Road, up Shamrock Street, along Lower Mount Street, across the Woodstock Road, into Upper Mount Street and over the Albertbridge Road to the 'quality shops', as my mother termed them, and the proprietors concurred. There were times when I was on one of these errands when I forgot what I had been sent for, and had to return home to check. Too many other things would catch my interest *en route*, and the dreamer took over. There were also those times when I would mistakenly enter the green Maypole instead of the red Dunlop's, and ask for 'Green Label tea', at the same time testing them with 'Spanish butter'. Memories can play tricks and mine was one of the trickiest. By then, of course, I was a loner, with no fatherly guide.

Past these two shops was The Mount, an area of distinction, where large Victorian houses climbed a hill to look snootily down their drainpipes on the three busy arteries below – the Albertbridge Road, Castlereagh Street, and the Mountpottinger Road. Robert Lynd, the great essayist, lived there, and off the Mountpottinger Road, in Madrid Street, was the residence of St John Ervine, the famous playwright. There, at the corner of Castlereagh Street, was a mounting stone, which,

My father Willie,
c. 1897

so I was informed, had been used by people of an earlier time to get on their horses. However interesting these facts may have been – and my father was never short of interesting information – they usually took second place in my mind to a more fascinating and immediate fact. Felix the Cat and Charlie Chaplin lived on the Mountpottinger Road. They lived in a big house called the Picturedrome and, as likely as not, my dad and I would be paying them a visit.

The Picturedrome was another world. Red plush seats that I had to be lifted on to, and where my legs stuck out stiffly before me, creating an unintentional hazard to those wishing to enter or leave the row. There was the excited babble of voices as people were shown to their seats. The smell of disinfectant was heavy and sweet, a male attendant loudly admonishing a group of boys and ordering them to be quiet. A sudden hush, lights dimmed, and a lady in the orchestra pit started to play the piano. Darkness. Then the curtains silently drew back, like well-trained lackeys bowing out, to reveal the magic rectangle. The tinkling piano was abruptly drowned by near-hysterical cheering as the title announcing Felix the Cat hit the screen. This early introduction to the silver screen was to prove addictive. The New Princess, the Willow and the Popular were quickly added to my regular haunts. That was the beginning of a great love for cinema, and later the live theatre joined forces with the cinema in holding me a captive fan of the Thespian arts.

From the first time my father introduced me to the Picturedrome and the world of films I was hooked. From Felix the Cat to Mickey Mouse, Chaplin to the Marx Brothers; from an old dear banging a piano to the world's leading orchestras supplying background music in stereophonic sound; and from the often soft focus and erratic movement of silent films to the magic of full-screen Todd A.O., cyclorama and 3D. What heaven it was for an addict to live through the unfolding of cinematic history. Watching the phenomenal growth of animated cartoons through the genius of the Walt Disney studios was to witness the development of an artistic miracle. On my first-ever visit to London, with my mother (who was treating us), Ian and Cambridge, we went to see the first great full-length cartoon at the New Gallery Cinema in Regent Street – *Snow White and the Seven Dwarfs*. Before the film was shown a cinema organist rose from the depths, playing tunes from the film on what looked like a giant multi-coloured jelly. It was all an exciting experience with which, in my mind, television can never compete.

In the early days, when the cowboy heroes Tom Mix, Ken Maynard and Buck Jones rode the range, when Warner Baxter and Janet Gaynor supplied romance, we got it all for one penny. Saturday mornings were the times and the Willow – or, to give it its proper name, the Willowfield Picture House – was the venue. We children held our pennies so tightly in our sweaty little hands that they hurt, and we would run so fast to the flicks that our feet barely touched the ground.

Excitement bordered on hysteria as we ran shrieking like an Apache raiding party along Cherryville Street. Up the entry to the cinema's back door we would race, pay our pennies to the woman who peered from a tiny slot in the wall, then clatter, half falling, down the steep well-worn wooden steps and in the door of wonderland.

In the half-darkness we would take our seats on the hard forms, which were the cheap seats. A red rope connected to two brass posts separated us from the red plush tip-up seats, which were the tuppennies. The smell of stale Woodbines and Park Drives competed with the strong odour of carbolic, and a general hubbub of childish chatter prevailed. Lights started to dim and, on the instant, the house erupted to shrieks and whistles and the stamping feet of half-crazed juveniles. The strong beam of the projector sliced through the darkness. Dots and numbers flashed on the screen. Music, like a gramophone running out of steam, gradually gathered momentum, becoming recognisable as the titles appeared.

When they built the Ritz cinema, on the corner of the Grosvenor Road and Fisherwick Place, it was acclaimed as the last word in super-cinemas. It was big but I would never have considered it super. I think Belfast's greatest cinema was the Classic in Castle Lane. To go to the Classic was to feel you were doing yourself proud; it had all the hallmarks of class. Its deep carpeting and classical design were richly extravagant, from bas-reliefs to the heavily ornamental double curtains. It seemed to ooze opulence, and a blissful contentment automatically followed. My first visit to the Classic was a special treat. I was taken by my mother when I was around six years old. Mother did not go to the cinema, as I remember, but she must have been curious on this occasion, or encouraged by my aunts to see this particular film – the epic *Ben Hur*, starring Ramon Novarro. Quite apart from the anticipated delight of the movie itself, my mouth sagged and my eyes widened when I drank in the oriental splendour of the Classic's décor. That first wonderful sensation of awe, which verged on disbelief, was unfortunately to be gravely marred by the film itself. Sitting with my mother in the front stalls, with eyes glued to the screen, I struggled to cope with the storyline, asking my mother what they were saying, as I could not read the subtitles quickly enough, if at all. The big moment came, that never-to-be-forgotten chariot race, when stunt men and cameramen combined to thrill you as you had never been thrilled before. In my case they succeeded more than others to date, with all their ingenious devices and cinematic trickery. As I sat there, one small boy, watching those flailing whips, spinning chariot wheels and sweating horses, I was in the Roman arena and it was real. Camera angles changed; the horses and chariots came charging forward, right at me; and over they hurtled, leaving me clinging to my mother with the wettest pair of pants in the cinema.

I saw my first talking picture in the Classic with Ian. It was *Bulldog Drummond*, with Ronald Colman – and that was his first talking film. This actor was to become one of my all-time favourites. His debonair manner, soft, cultured and slightly nasal voice made him a frontrunner from the word go. Many and varied were the actors I liked but Ronald Colman had that certain something over the rest, which to me made him unique. From the age of about fifteen I started falling deeply, perhaps hopelessly would be more correct, in love with one actress after another. There was Alice Faye and Ann Sothern singing love songs straight at me. Eleanor Powell with her gorgeous smile, and even more gorgeous legs, danced her way into my heart. The eyes and voices of Carole Lombard and Jean Arthur captivated me, but the one I was to love above all others was the lovely and talented Vivien Leigh. I thought her the most beautiful woman on stage and screen. I first saw her in the Imperial cinema, Cornmarket, with Rex Harrison in *Storm in a Tea Cup*, but nothing ever came of our romance, except perhaps that I did, many years later with my wife Yvonne's agreement, name our daughter after her.

As the reader will have gathered, the Lagan Village had not completely vanished when I was a child. A row of dark brown brick houses adjoined the Royal Bakery, on the opposite side of the road to our house. Its gleaming window panes reflected the Old Crow distillery and the schoolhouse opposite. The footpath outside each house door was scrubbed in a clean semi-circle. Opposite the shop where I was born sat 'wee white houses', as they were termed – history on my doorstep but, to me as a child, just part of my playground.

The white houses were much older than the dark brown ones and a lot smaller. A tall man could have touched the guttering should he have felt so inclined. At the end of the row and near the corner of Shamrock Street was Carrie Dunn's shop. It was a shop where you could get almost anything you needed, like one of those that still exist in the depths of Ireland's outback. Carrie was small, rosy-cheeked, and, like most of the villagers, a confabulator *par excellence*. She shared the shop with a sister who was in complete contrast – tall, thin, taciturn. Carrie's knowledge of local gossip, like her stock, was comprehensive and the knowledge she gave was free with every purchase. Should you want to know the way or the why, you would not ask a policeman – you would ask Carrie.

The 'wee white houses' were immaculately kept, but there was one in particular that shone out from the row like a freshly capped tooth. The lady of the house, little and plump, leaned on the half-door, her two fat and dimpled arms cosseting an ample bosom. Her twinkling eyes and friendly smile were constantly directed at the passing parade. Bonhomie exuded from that spick-and-span little abode. However, all was not as it seemed, because I heard it said that hers was a 'bad house'. This I could not understand, and I could only assume that the roof leaked or the plumbing was not as it should be. Maybe it had dry rot, or the foundations were in doubt, yet of all those little houses it looked the most perfect. Strange, too, that being bad it had so many very happy visitors. A constant stream of merry gentlemen, many inebriated, others not, paid regular social calls. Attractive and vivacious young ladies laughed and joked with the guests. The little house rocked with merriment of an evening, making its neighbours appear deserted. What could be bad about such a place, where happiness seemed so much in abundance?

3
MOTHER, AUNTS AND SISTERS

WITH HER FOREARM, MY MOTHER brushed the copper lock of hair from her brow. Some flour dust fell from her hand onto the crown of her head. She worked at great speed, pummelling and kneading the dough on the baking board. Hammering the ball of dough with her fist to flatten it, she took a rolling pin and attacked the rubbery mass to create a large white almost-perfect circle of dough about an inch thick. The sudden flash of a knife and a deft

crosscut action worthy of Zorro left the dough segmented. She immediately transferred the four pieces to the hot griddle, where the dusted flour was browning. No ordinary griddle this. To me it was a great black gloomy monster that skulked on its own table in one corner of the kitchen. It was a three-foot-square iron plate, one and a quarter inches thick, raised on a six-inch cast-iron base heavily embossed with a Victorian floral design. This beast was fed through a heavy gas pipe, keeping alive the little blue jets that danced underneath the plate. The griddle was at my eye level, and through decorative holes in the stand I was just able to see the yellow-centred blue jets do their rhythmical jig.

'Get out from under my feet,' my mother would say, as I fought for position to watch operations, and above all to sniff that delightful smell of baking bread. Like a dog on the scrounge, I kept getting in her way, hopping with excited anticipation of the delicacy to come – a slice of that newly baked bread with butter melting on it. To feel the chewy outer crust with the contrasting butter-laden soft centre in one bite was sheer ecstasy.

The soda bread, wheaten, pancakes and potato bread which came from that griddle tasted like no bread could ever taste again. Tatie bread was especially exciting, not only for its taste but for mastering the technique of keeping the butter from running off and down your wrists. Keeping it tilted mouthwards and curled at the side in order to have full flow control whilst eating was not easy. The bread, after all, was griddle hot.

My mother was a great cook and when she baked her cakes and mixed the batter in her large delft bowl, how impatient I would be, waiting to lick the wooden spoon and clean the bowl. I loved – and still do – that wonderful aroma of baking bread, and from my mother's griddle I would wander further afield in the quest for that seductive scent.

A balustrade surrounded the well in the floor. If I stood on my toes, I could see down to another floor. I did not like looking down: it made my head spin. From the balustrade hung massive carpets which smelled of dust. The whole place smelled of dust and damp. I hated this atmosphere that my mother seemed to thrive on. She dragged me here very often and also to other places that were equally terrible. Tatty old easy chairs, sideboards, clocks, prams, pictures, books, and a mass of other sad oddments lay in profusion awaiting acceptance like immigrants on Ellis

Island. My mother seemed to find everything most interesting and failed to appreciate how tired and bored I became. I yawned incessantly, almost dislocating my jaws, and dragged my feet wearily, reluctantly following her around, in and out of those mazes of mustiness, watching her lift, examine and discard, or falling over one of the depressed-looking men in brown coats who apparently knew so much. An almost-whispered conversation ensued, with 'tut-tut' and 'load of rubbish' and such interjections making themselves more audible than the rest of the exchange. These days were pure hell to me. They drained me of all energy, and appeared to have the reverse effect on my mother. Unfortunately, this was not the end of the matter, because that was only the viewing day.

Come the auction, I was again in close attendance. I gathered from the whispered warnings from the brown coats to my mother that over in the corner there was a race of people called 'dealers'. They, it would seem, were 'worth the watching'. One thing I could never understand was that my mother seemed to know the men called 'auctioneers'. These men got into a church-like pulpit and kept shouting about 'being bid' and 'making advances', all the time hammering the pulpit with a wooden hammer. I remember two of these auctioneers – one was called Captain Ross and the other Captain Nichol – and I also remember my mother talking to these gentlemen before the auction. What I could never understand was why, when the auctioneer had taken to his pulpit, and my mother remained where she was, they would keep nodding to each other throughout the entire boring proceedings.

Auctions, to my mother, were like bingo to other women. She was hooked. Many a bargain could be picked up at auction and sold at a profit to gullible relatives. She was a great woman too for discovering shops with articles that were selling 'for nothing', as she would put it to her victims. I can remember uncles with suits that were 'just made for you', and aunts with dresses and hats of a like nature. My mother never revealed who made them – which is perhaps just as well. The garments nearly always needed 'a bit taken in here' and 'a piece let out there'.

In some of the larger stores I would secretly learn to admire her business-like approach and at the same time wish I were somewhere else. The buyers were the people to know, I gathered, but could not quite understand this fact of life, because I thought my mother was the buyer.

'How much is this length of cloth?' Mother would ask.

The salesman, who really was a buyer, would examine the product. 'Well, it's an odd length, but it's a lovely piece of material,' he would say.

'I know exactly what it is – how much?'

'Seeing it's you, Mrs Friers' – darting looks in every direction, purely for effect – 'Shall we say two pounds, ten shillings?'

'If you like, but it's too much. Make it two pounds.'

'Well, now, I think two pounds ten shillings is the best I can do' – taking another look around. She half turned away and only just heard him say, 'All right, I'll have it wrapped, two pounds it is.'

The purchase duly wrapped and handed over, she would plant one pound ten shillings on the counter. 'That's all you're getting, you old robber.'

The number of times I had seen her do this and march off, leaving the buyer shaking his head, was impossible to estimate. Sometimes the buyer, having spotted her come in, would quickly get offside. But this ploy never worked; she would corner one of the salesgirls and demand to see Mr Blank.

'I don't think he's available, Mrs Friers.'

'Well, I'm not moving till he shows his face,' she would threaten.

The salesgirl would take one look at the determined expression and, feeling her own expression betraying her part in the deception, she would retreat with, 'I'll see if he's in yet', shortly to return with the heretofore unavailable gentleman rubbing his hands like Uriah Heep and wearing a sickly smile. No one could escape that single-minded fanaticism my mother displayed when on the trail of a bargain.

As a child, one of my very favourite places was the Royal Bakery and some of my best grown-up friends were the Stewarts who owned it. Their great horses I loved, and I often rode on them by courtesy of George Stewart, son of the proprietor. Some of the horses were stabled on the bakery premises, but the ones I rode were stabled in the entry off St Kilda Street. At my tender age, riding them meant that I had to do the splits when seated. The stable doors in the bakery yard took up two walls of a large square-setted area. It had the old-world atmosphere of a coaching yard and was part of the original Lagan Village. Of the two remaining walls, one was the back of the bakery itself and the other was that of an adjoining timber yard. The walls, heavily whitewashed, gave reflected light to what was a rather dark spot. The stables, when the top halves of the doors were open, exhaled that warm heady ammonia smell that sends a thrill to the nostrils of all equestrians.

The bakery, of course, had massive ovens – ovens from which white-suited bakers produced the fresh loaves with that mouthwatering smell. The heat in the bake house was tropical and you wondered how the men survived, day after day, in such conditions. It was here I used to watch, fascinated, the art of George's brother John as he created a wedding cake, weaving lacy patterns with icing, deftly fashioning roses in marzipan. I imagined him to be either a magician or the greatest artist in the world. I never tired of going to see John, just as John, so I was told, never tired of going to see my sister Edna.

A terrifying night was to occur during my young life when the bakery, my favourite retreat, its occupants and the horses were to be threatened. It happened with the suddenness of a bomb burst. The timber yard adjoining the bakery exploded into roaring life. An orange glow illuminated the village and people rushed from their houses to form a wildly gesticulating silhouetted ballet against the backdrop of dancing fire. Flames leaped high, straining towards the inky blackness of the sky. Bursts of sparks flew up, up and beyond, to vanish in the dark of the night. I could feel the heat on my face, and my trousers almost burned me as they pressed against my legs. My aunt Lila held me close to her. 'I'll take him to my house tonight. It will be safer,' she said. Red fire engines blocked the road and hosepipes twisted in all directions, like giant pythons. Great jets of silver gleaming water, alive with diamond sparkles, shot up into the inferno. Brightly lit faces excitedly watched the efforts of sweating firemen, whose own faces shone like their brass helmets, which reflected the mad dance of the flames. House and shop windows cracked with heat. Water from the hoses ran in red and golden rivulets, swirlingly glamorising that hell. Above the animated babble of villagers' voices the authoritative commands from the fire chief rang out.

'The bakery is goin' to go!' someone said.

'It is too,' said another. 'Look – the roof of the stables has caught.'

They were right. The insatiable monster's appetite was reaching for the bakery. Having anticipated that possibility, firemen and bakery workers had started to bring out the horses. Through the smoke the horses were led, their heads in bags to keep them quiet. Sensing the at-mosphere, they reared and whinnied, their hooves skidding and sparking on the pavings – strong, beautiful animals, pulling and tossing their heads to rid themselves of their hoods. Feeling the heat and hearing the crackle of the fire, they were absolutely terrified. They snorted and bucked whilst their handlers patted their necks, talking soothingly to them as they led them to the safety of the stables at St Kilda Street. I was taken (with less struggling) to my aunt's house further up the road in Rochester Street.

Next day, all that remained of the timber yard was a blackened wood-pile that looked like the remains of a bonfire, and the whole area stank from the black wet mass. Happily, the Royal Bakery remained intact, thanks to a highly efficient, quick-thinking fire service.

There was a time to follow, however, when some firemen did not fare quite so well . . .

To say my aunt had lost her composure would be a gross understate-ment. Her piercing shrieks cut through my semi-consciousness like rapier thrusts.

'Oh my God, he's killed. He's dead, isn't he, constable?'

The questions repeated incessantly, and intermingled with a baleful moaning, echoed and re-echoed through the labyrinths of my mind. Uninhibited and terrifying, like a banshee's wail, they had the effect of rousing me sufficiently to feel embarrassment at my aunt's pantomime performance, and also to make me conscious of the discomfort being caused by the constable's brass buttons pressing into me. The rough tex-ture of his uniform jacket felt like sandpaper against my skin. Then I heard the calm voice of my mother, strong and controlled, put an end to the cacophony of catastrophe. These sounds had been emanating from my mother's sister, Aunt Martha Todd, an excitable and dreary lady given to wearing black as though in morbid anticipation of disasters yet to come.

'Hold your tongue, Martha, don't be such a fool. Is he badly hurt, constable?'

'I don't think so, Mrs Friers. A lot of bruising and slightly concussed, I would say.'

'What on earth has he been up to, constable?'

This was typical – *he* must have been *up to* something.

'Well, he has been in a car accident, Mrs Friers. Not his fault,

28

of course.'

'What happened?'

'A car driven by Mr Alistair Kirk skidded on the tramlines and mounted the footpath.'

'Oh my God! Any others hurt?'

'As a matter of fact, there were about eight of them. A couple of broken bones but mainly badly bruised and shaken up. Lucky Bennett's gates were unlocked – it could have been nasty if they hadn't burst open. Things would have been a lot more serious if the children had been pinned to the closed gates. It doesn't bear thinking of.'

On this cue from the constable, I started to remember what had been responsible for my present position in the arms of a policeman, and what had caused the aches and pains I was suffering. My pals and I had been playing fire brigades, four tricycles, with one driver in full control acting as fire chief and in the lead. On each of the tricycles, on the back axle, stood a tail-end Charlie, holding grimly to the shoulders of the pedalling fury seated in front. Apart from being a fireman, he was also the bell and thus obliged to keep shouting 'ding, ding, ding' as we raced towards our imaginary conflagrations.

Through a haze, I remembered screaming tyres, shouts and shrieks, my tricycle flying through the air, then splintering wood, and blackness. Alistair Kirk's car had struck. The car was a Trojan with narrow wheels and solid rubber tyres. The wheels caught in the tramlines and the car mounted the footpath, putting paid to the charge of the light brigade. Bed rest for a week was prescribed to allay shock and ease the bruising.

Although reasonably obedient and looked upon by friends and neighbours as a good boy, there were those moments when I could be tempted to bend the rules a little. Such deviations could be assumed as perfectly normal reactions against a strictly authoritarian parental command. I was to be kind and considerate to all, obedient and willing, and never to use bad words. Any bad words I might have used would have been purely ungrammatical, as in 'I done' or 'I have went'. However, school and home soon rectified such solecisms.

When I did twist the rules a little, my covering-up was never successful, possibly because, if questioned, the fact that I was a bad liar let me down. On such occasions feelings were greatly hurt, mainly my own. My mother would say, in a voice that would strike terror into the bravest, 'Where are the tawse?' Tawse, to those who are fortunate enough never to have heard of them, was a strip of leather about two inches wide and eighteen inches long, cut into foot-long fringes. Expertly handled, they could soften up the hardest criminal. A sort of junior cat-o'-nine-tails, they must have come from the middle ages. I was not often the recipient of such punishment. The demand 'Where are the tawse?' entered my mind at the least temptation to wander from the straight and narrow. If or when tawse went out of existence, I never knew, that is, except for those in my own household. I remember my mother once saying, 'I wonder where the tawse have gone?' She had not intended to dish out punishment, it was simply that they had mysteriously vanished. Head down, my full concentration centred on the drawing I was doing, I smiled inwardly; the tawse were lying in that darkness between the wall and the bath where I had triumphantly buried them for posterity's posteriors.

A memorable time, indelibly etched in my mind, was when I attempted to steal money. My mother was hospitalised with an appendectomy, and home was under the reign of Cambridge. I discovered a vase in the pantry that contained cash – notes and silver, plus a lot of temptation. One quick check that there was no one around, and I plunged my hand into the jar and grabbed a fistful of money. Greed and dishonesty never really paid off, I learned, because my clenched fist would not come out of the jar, the fist's dimensions exceeding those of the jar's neck. Wrestling frantically, I was conscious of another presence. It was the custodian of the property.

'Why, you dirty little thief,' she hissed. 'How dare you steal and your mother in hospital!' The sudden image flashed into my mind of a poor sick widow and an evil, evil man stealing her all. The thought was lightning quick, but so too was big sister, who struck at that instant with a bamboo curtain rod. Opening my hand, I dropped the money plus the jar and fled towards the stairs, my bedroom, and sanctuary, the relentless pursuer close at my heels, the bamboo twanging with every direct hit – and few missed. Reaching my bedroom, I sought the protection of the bedclothes. Big sister, apparently unhinged, kept up the onslaught physically and verbally. I was made so aware of my crime that my future seemed irrevocably headed towards the gallows. From that day forward, stealing never dared enter my mind again. A lesson had been well taught and well learned.

4

PRIMARY COLOURS

I WAS A PERFECTLY NORMAL CHILD – I did not want to go to school. However, like every other normal child, I was made to go by grown-ups. But unlike most other normal children, this little boy had gleaned a lot of unwelcome foreknowledge by hearing big brother Ian and his friends talking about the Boyd Endowment and someone called Harbie. Now from what I could learn, this Harbie was not exactly the sort of person you could grow to love. Indeed, in my mind it seemed that Harbie was the sort of person you would like to stay well away from. Ian was a particularly good impressionist and his impersonation of Harbie conjured up in my child's mind a composite of all that was horrific in *Grimm's Fairy Tales* and naturally added to the abhorrent thought of starting school.

The school and Harbie were only about three dozen adult strides away from home, which added much to my discomfort. The first day for any home-loving child is a tearful one. To me, with the thoughts instilled in me by Ian and his friends, it was as attractive as the tumbrel would have been to Marie Antoinette. Luckily, I was not to meet the ogre on my first day, but instead a lady called Miss Faulkner, who was principal of the infant school. Yellowish of complexion, fuzzy of hair, straight of back, large of bosom, and bespectacled of eye, she was a disciplinarian but kindly.

The infants were on the top floor, out of reach of Harbie, who commanded the senior school underneath. My very first teacher, Miss Gamble, was to be an even kindlier lady than Miss Faulkner. Miss Gamble, as I found out, was inordinately fond of me, and referred to me as her 'little man'. She encouraged my drawing to such an extent that I presented all my lessons with pictorial adornments. This delighted her so much that she would bring me out in front of the class and show them my work. 'Look, my little man has drawn soldiers guarding his sums,' she would announce. This performance inflated my ego, making me feel that I was that teeny bit different. Psychologically, hers was an astute move, because when I became recognised as being especially good at something and accepted as such by my schoolmates, I almost started to enjoy school.

Miss Gamble's classroom had rows of seats tiered like the Roman Colosseum, and just as hard. Sitting at the back of the class, you had a semi-aerial view. For the first few weeks in her class, I sat at the back; it was only when I became her little man that I moved forward. Years later, when I was about eighteen, I met Miss Gamble in the city centre. I was looking into a window in High Street when a familiar voice hailed me from behind: 'Well, well, if it isn't my little man!' On turning round, the little man was surprised to discover that he was looking down on her. The last time I had had this experience was when I sat up there at the back of her class.

She was the perfect teacher for infants: gentle and kind, with never a cross word, just lots and lots of encouragement. She was tall and thin and eternally benign. Dressed for warmth rather than elegance, her taste ran to maroons and beiges, cardigans and woollen dresses. She wore flat sensible shoes laced tightly on her tiny feet, and her thin legs were cosily encased in thick knitted stockings. A small, round head, hair drawn back in a bun, surmounted a long, sinewy neck. Her pronounced Adam's apple travelled up and down the anatomical cables like a busy elevator. Her face was as lined as an exercise book and her rosy cheeks pouched like those of a hamster. Her granny half-glasses were clipped on the end of a nose that resembled a cherry. With large liquid blue eyes, she peered over the top of her glasses, slowly scanning the tiers of seats, upon which the few infants who had stayed behind during the break sat wide-eyed.

On a stool beside her were the remains of her lunch. With the utmost care she placed a square of paper on her knees, smoothed it out lovingly, then proceeded to fold it neatly into a smaller square. Next, she gathered her remnants, an apple core and crusts, from the stool, and these she wrapped in the prepared paper and, almost reverentially, placed everything in a brown paper bag. Then another piece of paper was produced with which she painstakingly proceeded to clean each and every finger, not forgetting both thumbs. That piece of paper was also folded and joined the dear departed in the brown bag. She proceeded to close the bag and then, after folding it to the smallest possible dimensions, dropped it into the recesses of her handbag. It had all the ritual and ceremony of a burial service. I watched these operations with a fascination that verged on a hypnotic trance. I wondered: why go to all this trouble? had she a use for this waste material? could it be recycled? Perhaps the edible scraps would end up in a bread-and-butter pudding. Having watched this ritual on several occasions, I remained baffled. Why did Miss Gamble not throw the lot on the classroom fire that glowed beside her, as my mother might have done?

The rest of the children had just returned and taken their seats a little earlier than scheduled, catching her before she had completed her tidying-up process. With a tiny lace handkerchief she delicately proceeded to dab away any particles of food that adhered to her mouth. Each crumb, real or imagined, would be deftly removed from the compressed lips, until she was satisfied no minuscule morsel remained. To complete the toiletry, she would withdraw from the confines of her voluminous handbag a small mirror which she gazed into, contorting her mouth in every direction to check the final result. Satisfied with what she saw, she replaced the mirror, snapped shut the bag, and ever so gently pushed it under her chair. Lifting a book near to hand and opening it at a place already marked, she adjusted her glasses, looked over them and said, 'Well, dears', and lessons began.

When the time came and I moved downstairs to where the demon Harbie lurked, I did so with apprehension, aware of his unenviable reputation for being a Wackford Squeers with a soupçon of the Marquis de Sade. This part of the school was more dilapidated than the upper regions. The walls, once upon a time, had been of that cream shade associated exclusively with old hospitals or workhouses. It was blistered and flaking from years of neglect, and the ravages of damp were making themselves felt. The lower part of the walls was clad in tongue-and-groove sheeting and painted imaginatively in brown. Just above the panelling, at a height of about four feet, rose tall Georgian windows that looked as if they had last been cleaned in that period. The floorboards were worn and uneven with a little woodworm hole or two thrown in for good value. From some of the loose boards, headless nails protruded at drunken angles, and knots erupted at irregular intervals, dark and shining like a timber acne.

At one end of the room, above a blackboard, hung a dreadful round-faced clock, which gave a loud clack every time the minute hand moved. During exams, that instrument of torture made the Chinese water job seem like a refreshing light shower. Facing the blackboard were two rows of forms: on the front row the lucky children sat, and on the back forms the later arrivals stood. Here Miss McMinnis taught, without teacher's pets and with great efficiency. To the left of the blackboard was a door leading to the hall, the outside door, and freedom. To the right was yet another door which led to the playground, high walls, and no escape. Her class was back to back with the class in the main room under the command of Miss Minnie. Miss Minnie was one of two sisters called Moore who taught in the school, the other being Miss Amy. Obviously, to have two Misses Moore in the school could be more than a little confusing, so in order to avoid such confusion the two ladies were referred to as Miss Amy and Miss Minnie – shades of *Cranford* and Mrs Gaskell.

The school was positively Dickensian with, although I could not have known it then, a hint of Edgar Allen Poe's House of Usher. Atmospherically, that may have been the case; structurally, however, the difference is marked in that, at the time of writing, the building has not yet fallen, despite the most ardent hopes of many of its pupils. Although no longer a school, it has survived the countless evil spells cast by many a miserable and unhappy junior. Ugly and dismal, a two-storey slab of red brick, to me and to all my friends, it exuded bleakness, and, to a degree, terror. A greengrocer's at the corner of Dann's Row leaned nonchalantly against the school's gable end, and the fresh smell of oranges and apples was the pupils' last sniff of the outside world before entering this, their purgatory.

Inside, the atmosphere was stale, smelling of pencil sharpenings and the wet pants of those who had no control over their bladders or nerves, or the combination of both. As you entered you were met by a wooden staircase, its treads worn in the middle with the passage of years and the thousands of tiny feet that had trudged wearily to the upper classrooms, or further, to the playground on the roof. This last innovation was the railed-in flat top of the building, and here, weather permitting, the youngest children performed 'The Grand Old Duke of York', or 'The Farmer Wants a Wife', and the like. To a small boy – to this small boy in particular – games in that rarefied atmosphere could never be classed as heavenly experiences. Here I got my higher education, and here I acquired honours in vertigo. Away down below, if I dared to look, was the playground for the bigger children, where they played tig and wrestled and the boys pulled the girls' hair. Altogether they had much more fun. Besides, I thought with a shudder, if they fell they would only skin their knees.

On one occasion I decided to mitch from school. This mammoth decision took weeks of preparation in building up nerve and determination. I kept it to myself. No pals were entrusted with my secret. It was vital that there should be no leakage of information, and that no one, no one but myself, should know the day or week I would strike for freedom. The morning I chose was not the best; it was autumn and a little dull, perhaps not quite as dull as I myself proved to be.

Only Doran's public house and McMullan's Lane came between my home and the school. I left home with about sixty seconds to spare before the school bell stopped ringing. With my school bag under my arm, I leaned down to tie my lace, thereby dropping the bag and spilling its contents. It took a little time to repack my bag. There was no one in sight, so quick as a flash I vanished into McMullan's Lane. I heard them singing their morning hymn in the school, and glowed with pride at my own daring. The hymn seemed longer than usual before the

familiar noise of pupils taking their seats reached my ears. Time started to stand still, and I began to think: where do I go now? The Ormeau Park? If I go to the Ormeau Park, someone will see me and tell my mother.

You really need company on a break like this. It is no fun on your own. All this time I had not moved from the McMullan's Lane side of the school. I decided to peep around the corner in the hope of seeing someone I knew who was not in school. When I looked I saw someone I knew all right who wasn't in school. Well, at least I saw part of her – her grey lisle stockings, flat-heeled shoes and dark skirt. I let my eyes travel upwards and there she was, as large as – well, to me even larger than – life – Miss Faulkner.

She took me by the hand and home to my mother, who was as surprised to see the headmistress with her son as I was to be with her. My mother's face told Miss Faulkner nothing, but I got the message that all my plans were definitely not going to work out well.

'Rowel has been absenting himself from school, Mrs Friers.'

'Surely not. He's a very good boy. He wouldn't do anything like that.'

'Oh, he's tricky,' came the terse rejoinder and, grasping my hand firmly, the headmistress turned sharply about and marched me schoolwards.

I often wonder how Miss Faulkner caught me. Was she just out checking for latecomers, or had she really intended skipping off herself? My total period *in absentia* was about fifteen minutes, but I was never, ever, to attempt such daring again.

Miss Amy taught the most senior of the school's infants, in a room off the main downstairs area. Her classroom, like Miss Gamble's, owed much of its design to the Roman Colosseum. There was a mean-looking little fireplace with a large wire fireguard around it, and outside, in the big main room, dwelt its brother, not a lot bigger and no less mean. During the winter these fires were sparingly supplied with coal, which would glow fitfully, promising heat but never keeping that promise. It was at this period, when tiny teeth chattered like castanets, that the school doctor timed his unwelcome appearance. The breaths of the pupils hung in the air like dry ice when the 'tick man' inflicted his humiliating strip show on us. A bunch of youngsters huddled round the pathetic fireplace, each awaiting his or her turn for examination. The search for alien bodies, or ailing ones, was on. We crowded together for heat, like day-old battery chicks around the lamp.

It was on one of these inspection days, as I was dressing, that on impulse I raised a hand. 'Sir,' I said to a white coat, 'please, sir, somebody's taken my pink combinations.' That was a big word for me, and I liked it. I also had the feeling that pink combinations were the last word in sartorial elegance.

'Where were they, boy?'

'Sir, they were on the fireguard.'

Nearly all the rest of the boys had dressed, some having rejoined their classes. A hasty search was set in motion, but no pinkies came to light. All those boys who had already been inspected were recalled and ordered to undress. Shivering bodies and icy glares surrounded me. Alas, their duds were shed to no avail. There were scruffy vests, and grey combinations, short-sleeved, long-sleeved, no-sleeved, and holey – but

no pink ones. Sherlock Holmes could not have helped that day. The school sent an apology to my mother for the loss. She informed them that I had never had pink combinations and that I was being funny. That was my first essay into sick humour.

In the big room, Miss Minnie's class sat at desks regimentally arrayed, and here she patrolled up and down the ranks, like royalty inspecting the troops. Each desk had a heavily engraved surface bearing the initials of those who had passed before and, without doubt, many who had failed. At the end of this large room and facing Miss Minnie's class, HE sat. He sat on a raised platform behind a heavy table, whereupon rested the detested school handbell, and that most feared of all things detestable, a bamboo cane tightly bound with fine twine at the end. A clutter of papers also lay on the table, a large ink pot with pen protruding, and some exercise books stacked eccentrically in one corner. As a head-master, he was as popular with the boys and girls as mumps: he appeared to have the same affection for children as they had for him. Wire-framed glasses balanced uneasily on the end of his thin nose, and a pair of ice-cold pale blue eyes glinted malevolently over them, perpetually scanning the room as a lighthouse does the ocean. He had a charming habit of noisily grinding his teeth. The hair, yellowish grey and thinning, was plastered down on a dried and chalk-covered skull, resembling the dank grass you find under a stone. Chalk dust also lay on his shoulders and in the creases of his shabby grey waistcoat. A large gold watch chain swung from pocket to pocket, and he would produce his silver hunter from time to time, checking it against the school clock to ascertain that the clock had not dozed off. His boots, turned up at the toes, shone like blackberries and squeaked when he walked.

He was religious to that extreme where a smile might be construed as sinful indulgence, and with radar ears he would stiffen to attention at the slightest unwarranted rustle or titter. Should it come from the class at the back of the room, he would rise stealthily from his chair and tiptoe down from his elevated post. Like springbok when a lion is approaching, the whole herd of children would freeze in their awareness of impending danger. Never were books more deeply scrutinised. Only extremely daring pupils would venture to move their eyeballs sufficiently to ob-serve the hunter stalk his prey. Though his ears were tuned to alien sounds, he appeared deaf to the fact that his boots squeaked like a rusty gate. Cane at the ready, teeth grinding in anticipation of the kill, he would move cat-like towards his target. Tiptoeing on his turned-up boots, he concentrated hard on a silent approach that was non-existent, his movements so exaggerated that his progress resembled some grotesque ballet. Added to his squeaking boots, a groaning floorboard or the metallic ping of a heel protector against a risen nail would telegraph both the distance and speed of his approach to the class in his sights. They would freeze in a hypnotic trance as they awaited the inevitable.

Suddenly, the fiend would pounce. Down would sweep the cane on a book held by the nearest target, the book would crash to the floor, signalling the start of an all-out offensive. With sabre slashes the cane would go to work; no back of leg or backside would be spared. Miss Minnie could just look on in horrified amazement as the class, before

her eyes, fell before the onslaught, a class which, up until that moment, she was confident she had in full control.

A haranguing verging on the manic would follow the slaughter of the innocents and several unfortunates, chosen at random, would be commanded to 'go to the corner' – a chilling prospect even to the bravest. The dreaded corner was a cupboard area adjoining the headmaster's throne, a throne where the cane was his sceptre and his motto was certainly not 'spare the rod'. Once he had someone in the corner, he could, and did on many occasions, let the victim stand for up to half an hour to suffer in mind what he could expect to receive in the flesh.

On one memorable occasion a boy who had been 'cornered' for some misdemeanour, committed or imagined, cracked under the strain of waiting. When the executioner arrived with his beloved cane, he was met with a heavy boot on the right shin. As he dropped his cane to nurse the shin, another kick landed on the left shin, swiftly followed by a blow on the head with a heavy school bag, which contained, amongst other things, a slate. Leaving the master 'smitten through the helm', the boy tucked his bag under his arm and triumphantly marched out of school to the very silent admiration of all witnesses. Oddly enough, he never returned to the school.

Harbie – or Mr Harbinson to give him his proper name – must have tortured his staff as he did his pupils. He insisted on launching his guerrilla warfare and attacked as and when his mood dictated. Often, after the morning hymn, he would move amongst the petrified children, looking for a likely victim. Having made his selection, he would grab a child by the ear, and the question would come in a menacing stage whisper more akin to the hiss of a snake than human communication.

'Did you say your prayers this morning?'

'No, sir', would come the tremulous answer.

'Why not?' – hitting the desk with his cane so that the ink hopped out of the well, leaving globules of blue.

'I forgot, sir.'

'You forgot, did you? Who gave you your breakfast?'

'Me ma, sir.'

Another bang on the desk. 'She did not, ye gull ye. It was the Lord gave you your breakfast, and He didn't forget – He never forgets, boy' – giving the ear a vicious tweak.

40

'No, sir,' yelped the boy, at the same time firmly convinced that it was his mother who had given him breakfast, his young mind unable to cope with a white-bearded man in a long white habit wielding the frying pan.

Harbie had a very nasty habit of confiscating your pencil if it were a Royal Sovereign or a Venus, and replacing 'that painted trash' with 'a good school pencil' – a mass-produced plain wood economy issue, whose only embellishment was the impress HB. Some of his pupils took this to stand for Harbie Balls, a much-used title bestowed on the head when he was out of earshot. When I was about three years old and had not yet started school I used to hear Ian and his friends refer to the head as oul' Harbie Balls. I was too young, and had too much admiration for my brother, to doubt that this was anything other than the correct name for a man whose appearance I had no idea whatsoever about.

When Ian was about thirteen he was good enough to take me to a show called *Limelight Views*. The programme, a series of slide projections, had been organised by the church and took place in a corrugated mission hall in Ballarat Street. Naturally enough, it was a religious meeting. The hall filled up rapidly with big folk dressed in their Sundays. The smells of piety filled the air – lavender and camphor. There was the usual excited babble of expectancy preceding lights out. His reverence mounted the rostrum, held up his hand for silence, and with bowed head and clasped hands prayed aloud in a mournful voice. Suddenly the hall was plunged into darkness and, equally suddenly, a beam cut through the blackness and a full-colour picture appeared, with lettering underneath it, and it seemed to just hang there in the air. The audience sang hymns and things were going swimmingly, the audience fairly overflowing with fervour and the spirit of holiness.

Then it happened. There was a break between hymns, and up flashed the picture of a wise-looking old gentleman with long white hair and a very long beard. He held aloft what looked to me like a big book. The audience gasped admiringly and you could have cut the atmosphere of reverence with something sharp. Excitement took hold of me and suddenly I started to jump up and down, shaking my hands. All my instincts told me I was right. I knew who he was. At the top of my shrill little voice I released my emotions with all the feeling that only a great actor could attain.

'That's oul' Harbie Balls!'

41

Silence, then a wave of nervous giggling filtered round the darkened hall. I only remember a door opening rather fast, a vice-like grip on my hand, and a red-faced brother escorting me home at a speed far in excess of my legs' capabilities.

I acquired much useful knowledge at the Boyd Endowment. I learned on the school-roof playground that I was more advanced than my classmates where vertigo was concerned, that the farmer wanted a wife, that the grand old Duke of York had ten thousand men whom he kept marching up and down a hill, that when they were up they were up, and when they were down they were down, and as a corollary, when they were only halfway up, they were neither up nor down. Why he acted like this I was never told, so my conclusion was that he was either fitness-mad or else a complete bamstick (a title often conferred on myself when the big brothers thought I was being stupid). I learned, too, that mitching was a definite no-no; that I never wore pink combinations; that Miss Gamble loved me; that I was not destined to become an academic.

I learned eventually, and on recollection, how good all my teachers were, except for the religious sadist who sat on his platform, gimlet eyes scanning the gulls (his expression, not mine) like some great bird of prey ready to swoop.

5

VIGNETTES

I OFTEN WONDERED WHY SAMMY COULD not play like the rest of us. Why were his arms and legs so skeletal, and why was he that purple colour, with such dark blue lips? Sammy would sit on the ground wherever he was and watch the rest of us at play, his eyes sad, and his breathing very rapid. His head, which appeared too heavy for his neck, rested on the arms clasped around two bony knees. Often, as those sad eyes scanned the animated and vociferous revellers, a strange silence would descend on us boys. We would stop in the middle of whatever boisterous antics we were up to, and suddenly, as one, become conscious of those sad eyes. Some would wander off, whilst others would sit down beside their watcher and start a storytelling session. Sammy died very young. Looking back through the years makes that picture more tragic, because had medicine then been as it is today, a comparatively routine operation could have cured Sammy, who was a 'blue baby'.

'Any oul' rags, bones or bottles,' he shouted hoarsely, as he led his donkey along the street. His small cart was piled with old clothes of all varieties and colours. Bones and bottles rested in a box at the back of the cart, partly covered by some of the rags. The little cart with its metal-rimmed wheels rattled over the street, lending a characteristic background noise to that hoarse voice. The rags, I was told, were used to make paper, the glass, naturally, was melted down, and the bones were used to make glue. Recycling in the twenties!

In another street, a man with a steamy cart would be shouting 'Fresh coal breek! Coal breek! Fresh coal breek!' The bricks – steaming cubes of compressed coal dust about six inches square – were a popular cheap form of heating at the time.

'Any oul' raws! Any oul' raws! Any oul' raws!' – that was the skin man, or refuse collector. Usually this character would be pushing a handcart, and his quest was for potato peelings and kitchen waste to be used for feeding pigs.

'Herns alive! Herns alive!' shouted the fish man. The herrings, in fact, were not alive. He was merely trying to emphasise the freshness of his 'Ardglass herns'.

'Sharpen yer knives! Sharpen yer knives! Any scissors, any scissors!' – that was the knife grinder on his bicycle-cum-grinding-machine, a Heath Robinson contraption which he pushed around. The bicycle had a wooden framework that housed sandstones, and once he propped the machine up, he would take to his saddle and pedal furiously, setting the sandstones in motion. Sparks would fly as he expertly ground the housewives' tired equipment into keen and potentially lethal weapons.

There was one character who wheeled a handcart with a super-structure in the form of a roof and four uprights, one at each corner of his cart. Balloons, red and white striped sticks with coloured paper streamers attached, and windmills – star-shaped pieces of celluloid on sticks – decorated his cart. It was generally well filled with jam jars at the end of the journey, and its adornments were depleted or completely gone, having been handed over to children in exchange for jars.

44

'Lavender, sweet lavender,' if it ever was called, would only have been heard among the flower sellers at the city hall.

Happy Jimmy of the many coats appeared in the village at irregular intervals. A walking ragbag, with one tattered garment hanging on another, he was like a human onion. All the coats hung open to reveal a potbelly around which a rope was tied, which held up greasy dark trousers. The trouser legs were tied with string at the frayed and ragged ends, displaying the dirty mutton dummies (as we called tennis shoes), which had long since gone a dark grey. The uppers had parted from the soles, which made them appear to wear a perpetual smile. An old striped shirt without a collar lay open to the bottom of his rib cage. His sweat-stained hat with its convoluted brim sat rakishly on the back of the crazed head. He had a pale fat face like a boxer dog. His underlip was very red and constantly wet, and he slobbered incessantly, the rivulets of saliva running down the ready-made canals in his jowls.

'Give us a song, Jimmy,' the children would shout, and as often as not he would attempt to accommodate them. Poor crazed being that he was, his singing was more akin to an ailment. Occasionally, too, he would add to his act a stumbling little dance. Most times he would be seen sitting on someone's doorstep with his 'piece', or lunch, which he had wrapped in newspaper. At other times he might have been seen (though not too often) holding money in his hand and looking at it in wonder – a magical something which he could not comprehend. How did it get there and what was it for? You could have felt sorry for him, but that would have been wrong, for his world was that of the child, uncomplicated and without responsibilities of any kind. He was, after all, Happy Jimmy.

Another character who paid monthly visits to our shop was the 'Wee Snow Whites', a tall thin individual who, like many people topping the six-foot mark, hunched his shoulders forward. He had a long, tanned leather face, deeply etched with the lines of time. He carried a huge wickerwork basket filled with clay pipes, whose bowls were embossed with either a hand or a harp. Seldom did he actually enter the shop; he would just push open the door, stick his head around and immediately following the cling of the bell would holler –'Any af the wee Snow Whites today, mam?' I wonder how many of those wee Snow Whites he had to sell to make a living, because our shop had only one customer for that particular pipe. She was an old shawlie who bought a new pipe once a month, with two ounces of snuff and a plug of tobacco. To a child she seemed as old as time itself. The fact that she smoked a pipe authenticated my belief that she owed an allegiance to witchcraft. The silver moustache on her upper lip was brown-fringed through constant use of snuff, and this added further to my lurid imaginings. A black-shawled, pipe-smoking, porter-drinking snuffer was over-stimulation to the vivid imagination of a small mind. I was always ready for the off when the dark woman put in her appearances.

These were the days when commercial travellers abounded, paying regular visits to the shop. They came from tobacco firms and from confectionery manufacturers, like Barker and Dobson's, Sharp's, Cadbury's, Fry's and Nestlé's. Sometimes I would be given a few samples of a new product, but there were even better times when my mother ran short of stock and decided to visit Cadbury's showroom. Then situated in Royal Avenue, Cadbury's had an upstairs room that smelled like heaven to a youngster, with its heavily chocolate-scented air. Visiting this wonderland that displayed every possible variety of chocolate-related delight imaginable was bliss. Everything was exhibited, making the room resemble a jeweller's shop, and the lighting made the coloured foil wraps glitter like an Aladdin's cave. Best of all, I could leave this place with pockets full of free samples. Heaven indeed!

'Come on an' we'll go and see oul' Ellen,' some boys would say, when they were fed up with cowboys and Indians, or kick the can. It was a suggestion I always welcomed because older people were so very interesting. Old Ellen sat on her bed, a black shawl draped round her shoulders, and a tiny lace-edged cap clinging to the back of her sparse but glinting silver hair. The dishevelled bedclothes formed mountains and valleys about her. A patchwork quilt, multicoloured and multi-shaped, created an impression of fields bearing cornflowers, poppies, daffodils, violets, cyclamen, and dozens of other blooms, presenting a landscape of make-believe. There she reigned, a giant queen in a land of little people.

Ellen, in her nineties, had a fascination for me and my friends: her stories of the past, of horse trams, the Boer War, and life in the country, which the Lagan Village was in her childhood. I sat in wonderment, looking on this indestructible old lady smoking her clay pipe. She had a pale face, deep-lined like crinkled parchment, and a resonant and masculine voice that would boom out the greeting – 'Well, wee lad,

46

how are you today?' The stress she put on 'lad' made me feel smaller than I actually was.

The whitewashed room of her cottage was completely dominated by the large bed. A tiny window, begrimed with street dust, grudgingly filtered just enough light to reveal that the room was sparsely furnished. A small chest of drawers, the top of it laden with bric-a-brac, including an ancient clock that ominously and noisily clicked the time away, stood against the back wall. A large linen chest occupied all that remained of the wall beside the door that led to a passage and the back door, wherein a cat could not be swung – indeed, a large Persian might itself have had a problem turning there. The fireplace was a small black hole in the wall, where a large cast-iron kettle sat on the glowing coke. The room was warm and a heavy aroma of snuff hung on the air. On occasions, as she told her stories, a pinch of snuff would be taken or, more regularly, the pipe would be produced as a prop to play up certain points in her stories. Our young eyes would follow the movements of her pipe as an orchestra follows the baton of its conductor.

Remarkably Ellen, though she smoked and snuffed, never held terrors for me like the black-shawled woman who paid her monthly visits to our shop. Many's the time I brought Ellen gifts of sweets from the family emporium. She appreciated these small tokens, which were a very meagre reward for the knowledge she imparted and for the colour she added to my life and the lives of many others. I will never forget the memory of that rapt group of five or six small boys sitting on the floor or at the end of her bed. Their pale faces, eyes wide and mouths agape, were a study in concentration as they listened to the stories of another, enchanted world unfolded by that ancient and dignified old lady. The title 'lady' is not often applicable, but in this case it could never be challenged.

Another Lagan villager who passed our door as regularly as the Castle Junction tram was a very large woman with her shawl wrapped tightly round her. She wore laced boots and carried what appeared to be a child within the folds of her black knitted shawl. I always thought of Charles Dickens's Sarah Gamp when she materialised. Week after week, without fail, she would trudge past our shop, turn sharp left, and push through the swing doors of the pub next door. She presented her large tin jug and it was filled with porter. She would then wrap the child in her shawl again and march contentedly in a homeward direction. Mission accomplished.

They stood in small groups, huddled close, heads touching in their intimacy. Arms were folded characteristically across their bosoms, an inheritance from the age of the half-door. They nodded in slow motion, not looking at each other, but all eyes focused in the same direction. The silence of the street was broken only by their hushed confabulations, which hung still on the air like the soft chant of a distant litany. The houses, their window blinds drawn, looked like eyes closed in prayer. Here and there a blind would move imperceptibly to reveal the nose and eye of a curious but more introverted neighbour. One woman, a chubby left hand cupping an elbow, caressed her chins with the right, and took a furtive glance over her shoulder before parting with her highly classified information. Following her revelation, a few heads nodded assent whilst a couple shook slowly from side to side, indicating a 'my, my' or 'I nivir heard the like'. Confirmation and disbelief were in concert.

Some men loitered around in self-conscious groups, most of them dressed in navy-blue serge suits and wearing brown brightly shining boots. This ceremonial garb was normally reserved for the Twelfth, for Sundays, and for other important engagements. The occasional man would have a Woodbine cupped in his hand, a quick and nervous drag from which would ease his tension, eyes closed in ecstasy as blue smoke filtered slowly from dilated nostrils. Other men who did not have the luxury of blue serge stood ill at ease in brown suits or sports jackets and flannel trousers. The odd one, having made some effort to rectify his sartorial inadequacy, would, with conscious deliberation, adjust his black tie.

The street was filled with a strangely tense atmosphere. Emotions of fear and sadness were mixed with morbid curiosity. Silence there was, yet the ears, like those of a dog, seemed capable of hearing far beyond the normal human range.

'But he was lukin' so well, Martha.'

'Och aye, a big strong man, hadn't a day's sickness in his life.'

'It must have been a terrible shock till hur.'

'Aye, an' she'll miss the money – he had a quare good job, you know.'

'Some sort of inspector, wasn' he?'

'Aye, he was a meter man wi' the gas people.'

'They say that wee wummin Logan hasn't long till go either. You know hur, don't ye?'

'No, who's she?'

'Och, you're bound till know hur. She used till come up and down the street regular wi' a fox terrier on a lead wi' a wee tweed suit an' a calliper on one leg.'

'Right enough, I remember hur by the dog. What ails hur?'

'They say she has it – you know what I mean.'

'Not that?'

'Aye indeed.'

'Oh well, that'll be the finish of hur.'

Cancer was a taboo word. To mention it seemed to have the psychological effect of endangering the speaker's very existence. Similarly, if children playing in the street saw the 'fever motor', they would shout as a warning the dreaded word 'fever', simultaneously spitting out the infection they imagined they breathed in with its passing. The fever motor was a dark blue ambulance with blue glass windows which operated from Purdysburn fever hospital. It was a grim sight anyway, looking more like a hearse than an ambulance.

'Luk, Martha, they're gettin' ready nye.'

'So they are. Don't they keep them horses lovely. Ye'd think they palished them wi' Cherry Blossom, they're that black.'

'There's the caffin at the tap of the windy nye. They're pushin' it out.'

'Isn't it a shame they didn't lay him out in the parlour?'

'Ach sure, it's hard to think at a time like that.'

'Wouldn't ye think when they're building houses they'd make the stairs wide enough to get a caffin round them landins?'

'They build them for living in, not dying in.'

'They've got it down nye, nat without a struggle because he was a quare bit of a man.'

'Nat many wreaths.'

'No, but sure who can afford flowers these days?'

'Still, it's a lovely turnout. Wee Arthur there doesn't look at himself these days, does he?'

'Naw, and thon fella Smith is a bit yella about the gills.'

The hearse moved slowly off, the two black horses nodding their heads silently, as though in reverence. The top-hatted undertaker walked ahead of the procession of mourners right beside the black shiny hearse with its tortuous carvings and decorated glass sides resembling the style favoured by publicans' premises of the period. Dismally and slowly the melancholy cortège moved from the street and then, all of a sudden, voices became more audible, even animated. When the door of the house of the dear departed closed, life, it seemed, began again. Window blinds shot up, curtains were opened, light and life flooded back.

Another act in the theatre of the macabre was completed. A couple of bronze chrysanthemum petals caught in the slight breeze slowly somer-saulted towards the grating and fell into the darkness.

'Our Queen can tummle the pole,' they chanted as they skipped down the street. Leading the procession was Her Majesty, proud and grand in all her regal trappings of many-coloured frills and flounces, lovingly tailored in crêpe paper. A flash of not-so-regal knickers would greet the onlookers each time she attempted her tumbles. Her retinue, who were also dressed up, though not on such a grand scale, belted out her praises with all the verve and inbred aggression of their loyalist upbringing. The pole she was required to tummle was a brush shaft, borne at each end by the strongest of her palace yeomen. Sometimes a flawed pole could cause the sudden fall of the monarchy. This was the Queen of the May, the one the 'darkie' said he would marry, and the one who could do anything under the sun, even beat up a rival queen if such queen should be foolish enough to cross from one realm into another. She, it was claimed, could also 'ate a hard bap', though why she should wish to do so, I could never understand. Perhaps it was to show contempt or defiance at the utterances of Marie Antoinette, or maybe it had

something to do with the Depression. No doubt it all had some significance historically, but of that I could only admit ignorance.

Nearby some boys would be blowing ciggie cards. They would look up for a second at the royal cavalcade, then return their concentration to the game in hand, like seasoned gamblers.

'No bendies, nye. Keep them straight an' don't have them stickin' over the edge of the sill.'

'Who's bendin' them? Ah'm only straightenin' them, so I am.'

'That's all right for a yarn, they're aisier till blow over when they're bent at the edges, an' well you know it!'

'You think Ah'm chatin', donten ye?'

'Ah'm only warnin' ye till keep them straight an' away from the edge of the windy-sill. You know the rules – fair's fair.'

'Sure this is a ratten windy-sill anyway – it's all bumpy.'

'All right, let's fine anorn.'

They would gather their cigarette cards together and go off to find better match-play conditions.

'Hiya, Scottie. Hi, Willie.' They shouted greetings as they passed some other boys playing kick the can or relievo. A hoop race sped past them and shot up an entry, the hoops bouncing madly and noisily on the entry's cobbles. There were hoops of all varieties – bicycle rims driven with cleeks made from twisted bull wire, pram wheels on long drive wires, or car tyres belted along with stout pieces of wood. To every boy they were Bentleys, Rileys, Bugattis, Mercedes or Baby Austins. Each driver was a Nuvolari, Caracciola, Dixon, Kaye Don or Sir Henry Birkin, and every one a serious contender for their own Tourist Trophy.

The streets fairly hummed with activity. Multifarious games were being contested in every street, with an enthusiasm which could be equated to the Olympics. At some street corners the hunched-shouldered, duncher-capped legionnaires of the unemployed lolled, hands deep in pockets, Woodbines dangling from the underlips. They shored the walls and studied their newspapers intently. Knowledgeably, they would nod their heads, discussing future prospects, their deliberations deeply serious until an agreement was reached. Then, cash changed hands and a responsible member of the corner cabinet detached himself from the group and headed off to the nearest bookmaker.

Through it all, the royalists and their May Queen marched, oblivious to everything but their own majestic progress. As they reached their chosen hallowed ground, it happened – the Royal Command Performance. A rabble of chuckling and jostling junior Thespians would form a ring and launch into a playlet. Young voices in the high octave range informed the world, yet again, of the wonders and versatility of their queen. Once again that darkie said he would marry her and this time they excelled themselves for sheer volume. A boy whose face had been suitably blackened appeared from the circle and advanced to claim Her Majesty's hand, which was by this time as black as his own. Who was this darkie supposed to be? Was he the coal man, and if so, was it not a mite presumptuous of him to seek the hand of a queen, and one so talented too? I was never able to solve that mystery, but the romantic in me led me to believe that the darkie, like the frog in the fairy tale, would wash into a prince.

'Bet ye're afeard to go up the Big Turn!' That was the gauntlet tossed. There was nothing to be lost by the punter – no cash, no marbles, not even cigarette cards. Only the challenged could lose, and what he lost would be face. To go up the Big Turn was a test of courage, a traditional tribal ritual, sorting out the boys from the kids. The Big Turn, the entry to Glentoran Street, was a long narrow one with a couple of sharp corners. In daylight it was about two hundred yards long; at night it was about a mile long and darker than a coal mine, still and eerie enough to strike terror in a small breast. Bats, rats, ghosties and ghoulies lurked in its inkiness. When my big brother took me for a walk at nights he teased me perpetually about the menace that might well be hiding in the black surroundings.

Faced with the challenge before me, a poem often quoted on those nocturnal wanderings came unwelcome to my mind:

> Like one, that on a lonesome road
> Doth walk in fear and dread,
> And having once turned round walks on,
> And turns no more his head;
> Because he knows, a frightful fiend
> Doth close behind him tread.

I became conscious of eyes staring at me, all searching me. Trying to overcome the terror that gripped me and at the same time give the impression of being unperturbed, I casually asked: 'Have you all done it, then?'

'Aye, certainly,' the answer came in chorus.

I was taken aback. They nudged one another and grinned evilly, still keeping their searching eyes on me. I gave my impression of a nonchalant shrug. 'OK, I'll do it.'

'Come on, then,' they roared, and took off into the darkness of the Big Turn.

As surprised as I was relieved, I joined the stampede. Up until this initiation ceremony, I had been convinced that the boys had always done it solo. That was the impression they had created. Now the truth was out: none of them had that amount of spunk to do a solo. They ran so close together, they might have been roped. Bonds of sheer terror moulded them into a solid body, many-armed and many-legged, with all their voices raised in one ear-splitting crescendo of sound. As they flew through the dark, their hands sent bin lids flying, their feet played havoc with back doors – all this to dispel any evil spirits that might be loose in that tunnel of terror, or, more realistically, ensuring that the local householders would be informed of their presence and that, therefore, rescue would be at hand.

The nightmare race up that mile of tarry, tarry night, shrieking like the demons of their imaginings, must surely have left deep impressions on many minds other than my own. How important those childhood days were to us, when boys moulded one another's characters through their derring-do.

How unfeeling and callous the young can be was brought home to me in a most macabre fashion. A bunch of boys were making their way to their happy hunting grounds at the Greenhill and Craig's engineering works. While negotiating the sewage-contaminated stream that we called the Wee Lagan, one of the braves made a discovery. It was the tiny naked body of a premature dead baby. The boy lifted the perfectly formed little figure by one leg from the filthy stream. Holding it aloft, he pronounced in sepulchral tones: 'Behold Moses, because he was drawn out of the water.' It was a statement that made all but one boy laugh. Then, to make matters worse, he swung the little body around in the air and flung it far into the Lagan proper. The hideous lack of human feeling appalls me to this day.

6

RELATIVE VALUES

UNCLE TOM BEW WAS AN Englishman, an accident of birth he considered to be an accolade. Bumptious and self-opinionated, he was not over-popular amongst the clansfolk. He and his wife, Aunt Ruth (my mother's youngest sister), lived off the Ormeau Road in North Parade with their two sons, Stephen (we called him Peter) and Kenneth. They were all well tended by another of my mother's sisters, Aunt Minnie. Their house gleamed and smelled perpetually of Mansion polish, and Aunt Minnie, who was a spinster, seemed to have only one love in her life, and that was work. Before moving in with the Bews she had lived with Mother and Father. Our home, I was told, became the poorer when she left, following the death of my youngest sister Helen, whom she adored.

The Bews, being my nearest relatives geographically, accordingly became my closest friends, and Peter, Kenneth and I were inseparable. About ten years after Kenneth's birth, a third son arrived, who was christened Clive Stoughton Elliot Bew, a mouthful that fully reflected the pomposity of his pater. Clive arrived too late to be in any way part of our set-up, though I did become his godfather.

Those early days at North Parade were heaven. The weather always seemed sunny and each day was long and exciting. Kenneth and Peter, and their friends Rossie Good and Jack McCord, a quartet of fun-lovers, added much colour to my young life. Rossie's surname proved prophetic, as he was to become a canon, later a dean, in the Church of Ireland, an achievement which I am perfectly sure could not have been inspired by any of the group. Jack McCord was the younger brother of the inimitable Stringy McCord, who taught art in Methodist College and later became inspector of art for schools.

Summer holidays were often spent in Bangor, when the Friers family
and the Bews joined forces in pillow fights at bedtime. Morning and
afternoon bathing was at Ballyholme beach, where, unless you were
quick off the mark, you would have trouble finding a spot to park your
carcass. It was so popular that there were times when it looked as if there
was no sand, only people. Some way out in the water, about one hundred yards apart, two wooden platforms of crisscrossed planks, to which
springboards were attached, stood sentinel. Halfway between these platforms, and a little further out, floated a raft for the swimmers. Dark and
gloomy to my eye, they were never to succeed in stirring any aquatic
ambitions in me. The water was always icy, and friends and relatives, try
as they might, could never convince me of the delights to be enjoyed.
They stood hugging themselves, water to the waist with teeth a-chatter,
their blue lips making a farce of their utterances. I never could understand why they were so keen for me to share their discomfort.

Along the promenade the council had erected a long row of bathing
boxes with green doors for the benefit of enthusiasts. Here you could
hire one of their splendid navy-blue cotton bathing costumes,
emblazoned with the white letters BBC. This stood for Bangor Borough
Council not, as I thought, for Ballyholme Bloody Cold. The people
who wore these costumes were either most courageous, highly
uninhibited or had no sense of pride whatsoever. They had shoulder
straps which were either too tight on your shoulders or else slipped off
seductively. A smart curved neckline was the epitome of discreet tailoring and revealed absolutely nothing to cause scandal and the legs were
long enough to reach an inch or two above the knees. They fitted loosely,
both in terms of design and in being described as bathing costumes.

'I can't get you all in!'

Many and varied were the changes that took place in these suits once
the wearers took to the water. You could dive in, and the sudden in-
rush of water to the suit would take you from being a seven-stone
weakling to having the proportions of a hippo. Ladies would hold onto
their shoulder straps when dunking themselves in order to avoid revealing all. Standing straight resulted in water cascading from the armholes
and down the trouser legs, the costume suddenly clinging to the body
in one hundred and one shining wet wrinkles. A long shallow dive, in
a costume of the standard medium-to-large variety, could necessitate a
fast underwater turn to retrieve what you had started off with. Those
bathing suits had immense elasticity, and once wet, anything could

happen: you could have one leg down to your shin and the other four inches above your knee; drapes like theatre curtains could adorn your rear end; or you could have floating on the water before you a paunch that was forty years premature. Many a man might have had a sudden shock when he spotted his future on such an occasion.

A lasting memory for me was Uncle Tom Bew, with tremendous dignity, striding out from the briny, his head held high, water curving out in great arcs from his inflated suit, both legs of the costume covering his knees. As he reached the pebbled edge of the strand, all the water had been drained off, leaving him with the twisting and turning wrinkles clinging to his huge belly like ivy to a water butt. What little respect I had for him up to then suffered a major eclipse.

Aunt Maggie Hutton, my father's sister, lived in a red-brick bungalow on the Comber Road in Dundonald, near Belfast. It had been built by her husband, Uncle Jack, when they returned from South Africa where they had lived and worked for years. The bungalow was about as interesting as a Second World War air-raid shelter with slates on. Uncle Jack's years in the building trade had not added a great deal to his imagination. With a large tract of unused land surrounding the house, he could well have erected a kraal, thus indicating that he had picked up more than mere sunburn in South Africa. Aunt Maggie, like the rest of my father's sisters, Tilly, Annie and Lila, was tall, slim and proud of bearing. Victorian in attitude, she was given to wearing high-necked blouses with cameo brooches, long dark skirts and flat-heeled sensible shoes. She towered over her husband both physically and mentally. To me, as a small boy, they seemed a strangely contrasting pair. Uncle Jack had retired to such an extent that he hardly rose from his chair, and Aunt Maggie worked around him as if he were part of the furniture.

The only excitement in that house occurred when the Tourist Trophy race took to the Ards circuit and relatives congregated for a grandstand view of the cars hitting top speed on the Comber straight. The front garden of the bungalow was about six feet below road level, and Uncle Jack, with a rare flash of constructive thought and energy, set to work with scaffolding and planks, erecting a most effective standing area from which the racing greats could be viewed over the hedge. Eyston, Howe, Hall, and Billy Cotton (of band fame) streaked past us into the pages of racing history. That international annual excitement which brought fame to Northern Ireland and thrills to thousands was enjoyed by the builder's nephew through a hole in the hedge, but as the years passed, and he grew taller and taller, the view improved with the lap records.

On one visit to my Aunt Maggie's, my mother must have had an inordinate amount of news to impart because I became conscious of the decline of daylight and of an increase in my weariness. Though it was not the longest day of the year, it certainly felt like it. Then, at last, came that characteristic remark of my mother's – 'I'll have to rush.' In a matter of seconds, coats were on, headpieces adjusted and I, a small boy tightly held in my mother's grip, flew through the air, up the garden path towards my aunt's gate. The long thin arm of the long thin aunt was raised in a farewell salute as we shut the gate behind us.

The walk to the tram was a long trek for short legs and a weary body. Mother was never one to dawdle, so my pace was a mixture of jogging and low flying as her speed increased. Dusk had well and truly enveloped us when we reached the terminus. The trees on the golf course were silhouetted against the darkening sky to our right, and to our left the yews and the headstones of the graveyard loomed menacingly in the half-dark. This was the end of the line. The tram, its yellow lights creating its own faint aura, sat at the graveyard gates. The conductor, having transferred the trolley from one cable to the other, and the driver, having settled at the controls on the cityward end of the tram, were waiting silently for the moment of departure.

Mother pushed me onto the slatted platform and I made for the brass handrail on the winding stairway that led to the wrought-iron grandeur of the open area on the upper storey. I was stopped short by maternal authority and guided into the warmer, though no more comfortable, area downstairs. The seats, which were ready for the inward journey, had all their backs reversed. At the end of a line, once all passengers had disembarked, the conductor would walk up the passageway between the seats, and holding out both arms, he would slam all the seats back. The backs consisted of one slat of varnished wood joined to two iron uprights that were hinged to the seat itself, which was also made of wooden slats set about two inches apart. Luxury travel it certainly was not, but to a small boy in the 1920s it had all the excitement of a moon shot to an astronaut.

After a short wait and the arrival of a few more passengers, the conductor pulled the bell and the tram clattered forward. A couple of blue flashes from the trolley momentarily threw the graveyard tombstones into bold relief and then we were on our way. The conductor lifted our pennies, punched holes in the 'in' part of my mother's ticket, and did the same to the halfpenny blue that was my ticket. The ching of his punch, the jingle of the money in his leather bag, the rhythmical rattling of the wheels, and the gentle rocking of the tram increased my childish weariness. With my head resting against my mother, I fell into a doze. In my drowsiness I was faintly conscious of the exits and entrances of passengers, and of chattering around me, but it served only to add a dream-like quality to my snoozing.

It was not until the tram car reached the village of Ballyhackamore that I rejoined the world of the fully conscious. The tram had stopped still and the passengers seemed to have been seized with an excitement bordering on hysteria. Gabbling loudly they struggled to disembark. Had I been on a boat then, I might have worried, but my mother was beside me and I sensed from her composure that there was no impending danger. Everyone was asked to leave the tram, and it appeared that they could not do so quickly enough.

What was the reason for all these adults behaving like excited school children? Something was happening outside, and judging by the mood around me, it could not be anything minor or morbid, but must be something wonderful. With Mother, I joined the exodus. Everyone was looking skywards, pointing and chattering. As I looked up, some of the

more excitable had started cheering. There, sailing slowly and majestically in the evening sky, was a huge dark shape like a gigantic whale. It moved easily with a distant throbbing sound. Underneath hung a long cabin with lighted windows. It was the R101, that great airship, which, shortly after that night when it held us spellbound, was to crash into a mountain side, with all on board perishing.

7

THE TWELFTH

SOMETHING DISTURBED ME. something persistent, relentless, burrowing into my deep sleep, calling upon my inbred tribal instincts to awake. I gave a restless toss, pulled the bedclothes over my head and buried my nose deep into the pillow. Faintly, ever so faintly, it penetrated my subconscious. At first it seemed that my dreams were to be enriched with incidental music. Flutes played softly in the air like the pipes of Pan. The strangely muffled thrum-thrum of a big drum, like a heartbeat pulsing in a pillowed ear, added its contribution to the magic. Slowly, constantly, the fairy notes began to form a rhythmical pattern in my languidly awakening consciousness. Note after note fell into place with military precision and my ears transferred the message to my now slowly awakening mind. It was the Twelfth morning. No ordinary run-of-the-mill morning, but the Twelfth, the glorious Twelfth, commemorating William's triumph at the Boyne.

The bands were on the march, and Protestant hearts were bursting with pride on their biggest day of the year, when every Orangeman marched as though he personally was just returning from defeating the forces of the papist James. I estimated that the band must be on the Lagan Embankment, or Boulevard, as it was more commonly called (some of my friends pronounced it 'voulevard'), the music fast approaching the Ravenhill Road. Turning over on my back, I listened to the rousing strains of 'The Sash' growing louder by the second. Must be from the Ormeau Road, I thought, a lodge making its way to meet up with some brethren at Albertbridge Road Orange Hall. Through 'The Sash' I could hear the strains of 'Abide With Me'. Must be another lodge and a band coming down My Lady's Road, was my reasoning. Then yet another intruder, an accordion band with 'We'll fight for no surrender'.

There was a time when to me it was Nosurrender, which I took to be a place like Derry, Aughrim, Enniskillen and the Boyne.

The bands were now virtually on my doorstep, so I hopped out of bed and looked out the attic window. As I leaned out, my pyjama trousers slipped down, exposing my buttocks. A swift tug and they were almost up to my oxters. I peered out to the right and there they were – the flying banners, the glinting instruments of the bands, and the bowler-hatted, white-gloved, navy-serge-suited and brown-booted Orange-sashed gentlemen of the order, no brother's tailoring outdoing another, highly respectable, dignified and erect, they marched to the rhythm of their bands. Occasionally, one of them might deign to give a regal nod of the head to an onlooker known to him, and no doubt already approved of by his brethren as an acceptable outsider. The swordbearers and deacon pole-carriers stepped out with all the demeanour of generals, now and then taking a peep at their pride and joy – the banner. Most of these, I was to learn later, were painted by a Mr Bridgett, a craftsman specialising in that particular art form. This knowledge I gleaned from the son of the said gentleman, whom I met at art college some years later. Many and varied they were: gold, silver, orange, purple, blue, all the colours and more than could have adorned Joseph's coat. From portraits of William in battle, to Queen Victoria and her Bible ('the secret of England's greatness'), churches, angels, the Rock of Ages, memorial portraits to worshipful brothers who had passed on to that higher and grander lodge in the sky, it was a travelling art exhibition, before anyone dreamed of the Committee for the Encouragement of Music and the Arts or the Arts Council.

In those childhood days it took five hours for the Orange procession on the Twelfth of July to pass a given point on its way to the Field at Finaghy. The Orangemen were all well turned out and orderly, dressed in their 'Sunday-go-to-meetings'. There were no macho men with long hair, tattoos and jeans. All the bands marched with a precision that would have done justice to a military march past. From the flute bands to the kilties, 'not a foot went wrong nor a note flat'.

One supreme recollection is of a country lodge returning from another townland where the celebrations had been hosted. When they started out they were led by His Majesty King William on a dapple-grey. William, pointing his sword defiantly heavenward, led his men to battle with an assurance worthy of d'Artagnan. Though hardly historically accurate in every detail, his uniform was acceptable to all but the purist. Perhaps one could admit to a certain amount of antipathy towards his work-a-day wellies – without doubt a jarring note. Nevertheless, despite any flaw in his royal raiment, his mind was fixed in the period. Proudly he led his men to glory, and if ever a leader was born, this was he.

The return journey was one of obvious triumph. Flushed from a successful day at the Field, with fresh air, good fellowship and brews, they marched homewards with chins, where possible, held high. Some had their jackets slung nonchalantly over one shoulder. Here and there a tie hung crookedly from an open shirt collar, and an odd sash had changed position – no longer *de rigueur*. The battle had yet again been won and William's conquering heroes were returning. A kaleidoscope of colour – the brilliant uniforms of the bands and the glory of silken banners dancing in zigzag rhythm to the rousing music – added firmness of purpose to the multitude of boots marching muddied from the damp Field. In the midst of his warriors, William sat astride his trusty, but now bored, steed. He had dropped back from the lead he held on the outward journey and was showing obvious symptoms of bottle fatigue. His hat sat at a rakish angle on a wig, now worn peek-a-boo style, and with sword pointing earthwards Billy drooped forward, nose almost buried in the horse's mane. A loyal brother on either side of the mount kept steadying hands on His Majesty, thus ensuring that he remained, if not upright, at least mounted. The Prince of Orange had revelled in the bottle, but now neither the papist James nor anything else troubled his happy mind. His Majesty's immortal memory had deserted him, and 1690 to him could just as well have been a phone number.

8

TENDERFOOT MEMORIES

THE JOURNEY TO MANHOOD STARTS when you are referred to as a 'big boy', no matter how much of a crowl you may be. A 'big boy' usually joins the Cub Scouts or its equivalent. I was no exception. I joined the 2nd Belfast Troop and promptly donned my uniform, from garter tabs to woggle, and Lord Street became headquarters. Though I enjoyed wearing the uniform, I was never really cut out for uniformity. I liked the campfire weekends in Stormont Woods, the bracken-flavoured tea, the companionship, and the sing-songs. Sadly, my ambition never stretched to badges, nor to the glory of being a senior sixer. When eventually I grew to that age which dictates progression either to obscurity or scouthood, I chose the scouts. Those were the days when scouts looked like extras from *Rose Marie*, with that distinctive Mountie hat. I moved from Lord Street to the scout hall at Cregagh Presbyterian Church, from the green scarf of the 2nds to the yellow and brown of the 66ths. My patrol was the Peewits – a title I always had strong reservations about.

The motto 'Be Prepared' was never more strongly adhered to than when I was dressing to attend my troop nights. The rapt attention to preparations would have sent Beau Brummell into ecstasies. Scarf freshly ironed and fleur-de-lis embellishment a-gleam on my woggle, my mirror image reflected the concentration essential to ensure that precise angle of the hat I was so proud of. From shining shoes to the point of my hat, I was utter perfection, ready to do any good deed forced upon me. On my scout staff I had carved a snake curling round from bottom to top, unintentionally creating religious connotations, as in Saint Patrick, or Aaron and his rod. The short, neatly creased trousers were held up by a strong leather belt. From this hung a collection of implements to cope with any emergency. One of these, of which I was particularly proud, was a large clasp knife that Ian had given me. All you could ever want was built in. When fully opened it resembled a metal hedgehog, everything from that mundane 'thing for removing stones from horses' hooves', to instruments so sophisticated and abstract in shape that even the scoutmaster could not fathom their purpose. In the unlikely event of this versatile and extremely heavy accoutrement failing, a horn-handled sheath knife nestled in my right sock. Being more prepared than most, and ready for the direst emergency, in my left sock I had concealed a smaller sheath knife. Should I have been arrested today carrying all I did then, the security forces would be claiming a major arms' haul. The one disadvantage I had with my belt arose during exercises. After jumping up and down – arms up, arms down, knees bent, and all that leaping around – the weight of my armoury used to bring my trousers down. This necessitated jumping with one hand going up and down, the other being utilised keeping my dignity up.

For all my appearance of the perfect scout, the pride of Baden-Powell (or Bathing Towel, as I knew him in the cubs), sadly, I was but a cardboard replica. All my troop were laden with badges – woodworkers, map readers, trackers, actors, neurosurgeons. Every badge it was possible to get, they had them. I had none. A lot of them, if not all in my time, had 'artist' badges; I was an exception, although funnily enough, the patrol corners were all decorated with my drawings. My ambitions never stretched towards being a commissioner. At dressing up as a scout I was without doubt supreme, but under that dressing, no salad.

Once, a summer camp to Tyrella in County Down was arranged. I saw a glorious and exciting prospect for adventure in the sun. Excitement verging on hysteria seized me. All the arrangements and all the equipment necessary struck me like a tornado. I was caught up in the whirlwind and my mind spun in confusion. A thing called a pally ass was required – not a friendly donkey, but a bag of straw, a sort of mattress. My mother laboured at this particular item and produced a most compact and comfortable bed. Lots of work went into the preparations and when the big day came I left home laden like a pack mule. Knees bent, I set forth, gripping my staff like a pilgrim, or perhaps more like one of those intrepid climbers who head towards the challenge of Everest.

Tyrella was bathed in summer sunlight. The beach teemed with cavorting, squawking humans. Beach balls bounced, dogs barked and chased madly hither and thither. Shouts and laughs echoed and re-echoed atmospherically in the still air. We set up one bell tent and a small hike tent behind some sand dunes. This was to have serious consequences, more serious than the scoutmaster could have imagined. The bell tent could only hold so many, but not so many as to include me and another young scout called McCourt. Thus it was decided that we should share the hike tent. That initial blow hurt me: I felt I was being victimised, but decided to take it like a man – perhaps a man out of work and with little prospects, but nevertheless a man. The day passsed, being spent with setting up, having a short singsong round the campfire, and so to bed.

The palliasse felt good and McCourt was a most agreeable character, full of chat. We talked until after midnight, with eyelids starting to get heavy. Unfortunately, unknown to us, the clouds outside the tent got even heavier. It started to rain; a gentle tapping on the tent gradually gathered momentum, building up to the sound of distant tom-toms. A drop of cold water splattered on my forehead, followed by a second and a third.

'Look where it's coming in and run your finger down the tent.' The instructions came to mind. This accomplished, all went well until McCourt found he was having problems at his side too. Before long our fingers were as active on the tent as a couple of harpists in concert. Thunder rumbled around and the tent was illuminated with the blue light of elemental electricity. As the rain got heavier, the tent started to leak at ground level. We crawled out into the night and started to dig a trench round the tent. No one stirred from the bell tent – good deeds were less of a priority than good sleeps. We struggled on and completed our task, then utterly exhausted, returned to the comparative shelter of the hike tent. Suddenly the rain, as is so often the case, stopped. A distant rumble of thunder sounded like a tympanic roll heralding the finale of a very tempestuous overture. A polite cough drew our attention to the tent opening. Framed therein was the smiling face of the scoutmaster.

'I wonder, boys, would you mind letting this gentleman share your tent? He's a cyclist and was caught in the rain.'

We could not say no – we were speechless. What looked like the proof of Darwin's theory crawled into our presence, grunted a form of greeting, and threw himself prone. A hike tent would have suited

him reasonably well – possibly as an anorak. However, we two boys finished what was left of our sleepless night like two crabs under a rock that snored.

Early next day, having stoically survived the traumas of the night, I confronted, or maybe, to be more precise, hesitantly approached the scoutmaster.

'Please, sir.'

'Yes, what do you want, boy?'

'Please, sir, I want to go home.'

'You're joking, aren't you?'

'No, sir. I want to go home.'

By this time tears, combining with panic, were not far off. Sardonically, the scoutmaster addressed me, superman to maggot.

'Cold feet, eh?'

'No, sir, my feet are quite warm. I just want to go home.'

The expressions on my family's faces were unforgettable when they saw me return that very day from the Great Alone, like a heavily laden sourdough, damp palliasse and all. Thus ended an undistinguished scouting career. The only badge I ever got was many, many years later when the Silver Badge of Scouting was awarded to me for the performance of more good deeds outside the movement than were performed when I was a tenderfoot.

9

PARK PARADE

MY DEPARTURE FROM HARBIE'S educational chamber of horrors, although not the happiest day of my life, could rate among the top twenty. Getting away from that atmosphere was as uplifting to me as it must have been to Smike on his escape from Dotheboys Hall. I had nice new books, with neat covers made from wallpaper or, in some cases, brown wrapping paper, a new school bag with the exciting smell of leather, and, of course, most exciting of all, a new school. Park Parade – at that time still referred to as the 'new school' – was too new for any of my brothers and sisters to have gone there. They had attended the Model School, an establishment that had an enviable reputation academically. Park Parade, a rustic brick edifice built in the style of the time, was beside the Ormeau Park. It had three entrances: one for girls at the Ravenhill Road end, one for boys at the opposite end, facing towards the River Lagan, and a third, which was much more impressive, was smiled upon by the Ormeau Park. This entrance was obviously for teachers, inspectors, men from the ministry and other VIPs. I was often to slip in that way myself, mostly to disguise lateness.

At Park Parade it was not long before I established myself as an outstanding character. By this it is not implied that I was out standing in the corridor, where miscreants were usually sent to sweat and await the headmaster's circumnavigations. No. That was never something with which I was to be troubled. My unique popularity sprang, not from my striking good looks or even my charm, but from that wonderful ability of being able to draw. The school was full of boys who could play football, were good at maths or science, and girls too who excelled at hockey and academic subjects galore, but could they draw? No, not, as they freely admitted, 'as much as a straight line', which accomplishment few professional artists could manage. To be thus singled out as something different by my schoolmates and my teachers was to lay foundations for the future. The importance of early recognition should never be underestimated. It charges the batteries for achievement, and the drive to do better and better and impress your admiring audience more and more was the ultimate desire. Anything that I may have achieved later in life can justly be attributed to the interest shown by my schoolmates, teachers and immediate family.

The Parade was huge by comparison with the school of my previous incarceration. It was bright and airy, with more facilities than the Boyd Endowment had loose floorboards. My teachers, in whose classes I dozed when not doing English or art, numbered eight. The headmaster was one Mr Charles Wilson, who had the reputation of being a very fair man. He also had a very good technique with the cane for those who fell foul of him. Happily, I was sent to Mr Wilson only once, for some minor misdemeanour or other, like not doing my homework. In fear and trepidation I went to his office and knocked gently enough not to disturb him. Should he not hear the knock, the ploy would then be to return to the class with the excuse that the head was not there. The head must have been endowed with remarkably acute hearing, because the bark 'come in' made the knocker's feet leave the ground. I opened the door, sidled in, and gently and slowly closed it behind me.

Mr Wilson, with his long aquiline nose, red face and sandy hair, was bespectacled and well dressed in a chequered suit. He looked up from his marking. As he put his hand to his chin, he almost upset a cup of tea which sat before him on his desk. 'Why are you here, boy?' he asked in a surprised voice. When the explanation was revealed as to why I was there, an amazed pupil was asked if he would care for a cup of tea. It was better than the cane, so the offer was hastily accepted. A cup was produced and tea poured from the small pot on a tray which also held a plate of biscuits.

'Milk and sugar?'

'Yes, sir. Thank you.'

There they sat, the headmaster, and the pupil with a shaking teacup. A long chat ensued, the headmaster expressing his surprise at seeing that particular pupil in his office. Some lengthy but kindly advice, and the extraction of a promise that the pupil would never again appear in that office unless, of course, he was invited for tea. And that was my one and only confrontation with the head. I had also escaped the wrath of Attila the Hun's descendant, Harbie.

Towards the middle of my period at Park Parade I had a class with Mr Wilson for stuff called trigonometry, a form of hieroglyphics used by the early Egyptians, I thought. How I got through the class without Mr Wilson launching some form of attack, I never could fathom. That head must surely have been one of the most understanding educationists of his day, or could he have been concerned about his blood pressure?

My first teacher at the Parade was Miss Donaldson, petite and pretty. I fell in love with her from the first morning prayers. Curvaceous and vivacious is how I would have described her, if I had known what those words meant. Her name was Florence, but she was better known to her pupils as Wee Fluff. Whether she herself was acquainted with that name has never been recorded. She had a very endearing weakness, which was making pets of some of her class. I was over the moon when I became a favoured one. Maybe she had caught the love light in my eyes. What bliss when she brought me out in front of the class, ran her hand through my curls, and asked me to draw something on the blackboard. She had lovely grey-blue eyes and darkish blond hair. I was nearly as tall as she; I came up to her bosom, and when she held me close to her side, I could hear her heart beat, but only just, because mine was, I firmly believed, heard by the whole class.

A rumour started amongst the older boys and girls that a dance was to be held in the school's central hall. Alas, it was only for grown-ups, the teachers and their friends – no chance of a fandango with Fluff. I recall the night of the ball with a heavy heart. There was a bright silver moon embedded in deep blue velvet, surrounded by a diadem of diamonds dancing. The school looked completely transformed that night. Lights blazed from within, and the VIP entrance spilled coloured light out onto the quadrangle. There had been some rain and the lights sparkled, creating a bejewelled entrance to the ball of the year. Cars started to arrive, and princes in dinner jackets escorted princesses in glamorous gowns in many styles and colours.

Then I saw her get out of one of the cars. She was radiant in a white gown. A necklace sparkled at her throat, but it merely twinkled, as she herself glowed in an aura of blinding beauty. My heart raced with excitement and I nearly wept with emotion. Suddenly, a tall handsome

70

man came from behind the car. She looked up at him adoringly, took his arm, pressed her head close to his body in a form of caress, and together they swept through the school gates and into the ball. They never even noticed me standing there, as the light of love glimmered and went out, leaving a large tear on each cheek. If Wee Fluff ever really taught me anything, it was 'la donna è mobile'. A few years after that school dance, Wee Fluff was to find real romance, which took her from the Emerald Isle to the United States of America.

My next teacher was a very different lady indeed, much more mature in every way. At the age I was then, I would have imagined her to be long overdue for retirement. She was probably only in her forties, but her pale, gaunt face carried many creases and she was very serious indeed. No pets in her class. It was noses down and concentration on the work. She had high cheekbones, a tight mouth, and a chin that said clearly that the lady was determined. Her hair was curly and fuzzy, fairly dark, but giving the appearance of being covered with a light frost. She held herself straight to such a degree that the class nicknamed her the Sergeant Major. Class discipline was rigid enough to strengthen the military rank bestowed by her pupils.

Others of the tutorial team ordained to mould my future were Miss Irvine, who was both lovely to look at and delightful to know, and Miss Brand. Miss Brand, or Firebrand, in my young mind could have made a better career with HM Prisons. Once, after some rather dull answers to bright questions, she blew her top completely and roared (she had a deep voice) at her class of boys, and called us a lot of simpering girls. A sewing class was instigated and she produced needles, thread, buttons and patches. To give boys such lethal weapons, where you have itching fingers and other boys' bottoms getting in the way, is to beg disaster, and disaster it proved to be – that sewing class was a howling success.

I had only been at Park Parade for a couple of years when I started to have yearnings for elsewhere. Reading the *Magnet* whet my appetite for better things. The Famous Five and the Remove, the Cross Keys and Vernon Smyth made me restless and stimulated a strong desire to move on to those better things. I envied my cousins at the Royal Belfast Academical Institution and if I could not go to Greyfriars, the least I could do was to join them. I decided to sit an entrance exam, my ambition out of control and my courage quite unbelievable. Peter and Kenneth Bew wore school caps quartered in yellow and black. They also had blazers with a nice emblem on the pocket. I envied them the show just as I had coveted the pink combinations. So much did I want that gear that I had the audacity to try the entrance exam.

How well I remember that day in 1932. It was bright and sunny and quiet, and there was little traffic as I walked up Wellington Place towards Inst. I felt elated and also a little nervous as I clutched my pencil case, ruler, set square and protractor in sweating hands. The Black Man on his pedestal seemed to smile upon me as I passed. I liked him for that. Along the path beyond the side of the Belfast College of Technology I strode to the entrance of the great school. It was dark as I came in from the sunlight and the smell of school, just like any other school, filled my nostrils. I got a little less excited but much more nervous. When the exam started and the papers were handed out, the clock made its presence felt, ticking away loudly. I hate clocks: they may tell you the time but they do not give you any. The exam papers were extremely interesting. There were questions, cleverly phrased, which I could not answer. Had they been written in Greek, I would not have found them any more difficult. The difference in standards between Park Parade and Inst. was painfully evident and my vision of the yellow and black cap started to fade away. Art and English, I had little trouble with, but this, of course, had also been the case in Park Parade. One teacher at Inst., W.R. Gordon, affectionately known by the pupils as Daddy Gordon, was very nice to me on that terrible day. I was told afterwards that he had tried to get me a place through art and English alone – but that may have been someone trying to make me happy. Coincidentally, when later I was to go to art college, W.R.'s daughter, Maeve, was one of my fellow students.

We had, of course, our ration of male teachers in Park Parade, and a mixed bag they were too. Dutchy Holland was an affable but serious gent, who had a reputation out of school as a singer. He was said to be equally good as a teacher and, when necessary, could make use of the conductor's baton in class for unmusical purposes. I never experienced any of his particular attributes first-hand.

Sam Barbour was a disciplinarian who had a short, fast-burning fuse. He too had the reputation of being very generous with the rod. I did have experience of him and can confirm both the fuse and the rod. On the few occasions when he caned, I hastily and in agony would take a wild glance at the floor to see if any fingers were lying around. One thing cannot be denied: he was a good enough teacher to keep you from making a habit of punishment sessions.

With Len Moffat, school was fun, as long as his ulcer was not acting up. A good friend of my brother Ian, he may well have been easier on me than on others. (It always pays to have connections.) One thing that set Len apart from all the others was his superb use of chalk. He could throw it with great force and unerring accuracy at any inattentive head. I only recall him missing on one occasion. His ulcer was misbehaving at the same time as a pupil, while Len was cleaning the blackboard. He turned around swiftly, spotted the miscreant and flung the wooden duster. Fortunately the intended victim noted the action and ducked, and unfortunately for Len the missile shattered the school window.

Pat McAllister was bald and portly, sported a small grey military moustache and smoked a pipe incessantly, even in class. He regaled us with stories about the First World War and about how he helped to win it. He was a delightful man who introduced us to Shakespeare and gave us play readings from the Bard.

The youngest of all our male teachers was a man called Sam Cuddy. He was only ten years older than his fifteen-year-old class members. He was a man born to teach, one of that rare breed fortunate enough to find the occupation they were made to fill and to love it. He was really head boy of that class and everyone's pal. Being so close to a class can only make for success, and his was the best class in the school, and without any doubt, it was certainly the happiest. In those days, it was referred to as Eighth Standard, and it ended school life as I knew it. Now I had to look to the big world outside for a career, a career I could like. I wanted to find something that I was suited to, something that would make me as happy as Sam Cuddy.

Although I had my good times at school, I could never be so hypocritical as to claim them as the best years of my life. Park Parade, barring a couple of teachers, was dull and most decidedly never projected as strong a personality as the Boyd Endowment – which was possibly something to be grateful for.

10

THE WORLD OF WORK

IAN, REALISING HIS YOUNG BROTHER'S potential, organised an interview for me with the managing director of S.C. Allen and Company. Allen's was one of the great printing houses in the British Isles, as were Marcus Ward, and McCaw, Stevenson and Orr. London theatrical posters were printed here, and with customers such as the P and O line and Lyons, its clientele was phenomenal. Guinness posters piled in time after time: the man with the girder; Guinness for strength; the toucan; the ostrich; the seal, and many more. Guinness was good for Allen's. To join the company then was something special, a prospect to make the young mind spin. It was like being accepted by RADA or being made captain of the school soccer team, particularly as I could neither play soccer nor relate the comparative importance of football and acting.

Examples of my creativity in black and white and colour were duly collected and presented to the managing director in order to convince him that his organisation would not survive without this injection of my genius. He was a rather conventional gentleman, conforming to type – dark suit, white shirt with lots of cuff, club tie, horn-rimmed spectacles, and a holier-than-thou demeanour – and he bade Ian and I sit before him at his huge mahogany desk. The office displayed many posters, all representing the most valuable accounts. A brief but obvious peep at his gold wristwatch, a few essential pleasantries, and he skimmed through my works of art like a professional gambler shuffling cards. He knew as much about art as an elephant knows about a *pas de deux*. He removed the horn-rims, chewed the end of one leg, raised an eyebrow and, ignoring big brother, addressed his remarks to me, the boy genius: 'We start at 8.10 a.m. sharp, not a minute later. Start on Monday. Wages, six shillings and sixpence a week.' He looked at his watch once more, called

74

his secretary in to 'show these gentlemen out' and, creating the impression that everybody in the building needed him, he vanished through a heavily panelled door.

Rising at 7.00 a.m. to get to work was a job in itself. A quick wash helped to widen the eyes, then a quicker comb through the black curls, and downstairs to porridge and toast. A packed lunch was pocketed and I closed the shop door behind me. I had left my childhood behind for ever, and suddenly I was grown up, I was a working man. The way I was now heading was the road ordained. There would be no turning back, of that I was convinced. There were times at school when I thought I would like to be a monk, and such a thought was not idle fancy. I could never have imagined myself as an engine driver or a policeman, or anything so run-of-the-mill. Monks suggested tranquillity to me, a life of reading, philosophising and, of course, painting. Perhaps my surname subconsciously influenced such thinking, or maybe the fact that I always admired the plump and confident monk whose wisdom kept Robin Hood on the right path, or the fact that my schoolmates nicknamed me Friar Tuck, could have inspired such an unusual and highly original ambition in a Protestant child.

The sounds of industry wrenched me from my daydreaming, and a tram laden with dungareed men clattered past, its trolley spluttering blue stars. A baker's cart went by on the far side of the road and the bread server waved his whip in salute. There would be no more visits to the bakery to watch John Stewart create his sculptural masterpieces in icing sugar. A man would not have the time after a day's work. Over the Albert Bridge and into the procession of industry I went, pavements echoing to the marching sound of hobnailed boots, intermingling with clanging trams and the shuddering of metal on square setts from horses and carts.

On to the Sand Quay, where there were no trams, just the odd cart and a cavalcade of cyclists pedalling furiously, as though they were competing in the Tour de France. The odd factory horn wailed a warning that clocking-in time was near to hand. I stole a glance to my left at St John's Church and visions of the Reverend Charlie Maguire and Sunday school days flashed through my mind. The only men who went to Sunday school were the teachers; I would not go now. Though I may have had aspirations towards a monastic life, I most certainly had not been drawn to the religious life. I gave an involuntary shudder as I passed the

morgue on my right. The nearer I got to the place of my dreams, the faster I walked. This was in striking contrast to those first steps towards school.

Now a long line of Belfast Omnibus Company buses stood by the kerbside. The camber of the road tilted them slightly to port, giving them a relaxed and almost nonchalant look. The hustle and bustle of the Queen's Bridge raced towards me. A pandemonium of sound and movement was all under the control of a jolly red-faced policeman. His white-gloved hands fluttered about like butterflies as he directed the smooth flow of traffic, shouting pleasantries at all and sundry. He was a man happy at his work, tossing happiness around like confetti at a wedding. A grey mass of workmen teemed over the bridge Islandwards – proud shipbuilders all. Above them the gulls wheeled and slewed in a blue sky. Dazzlingly white, spotlighted in the morning sun, they added their excited squawks and honks to the industrial concerto below. The *Robina* and the *Smeaton*, lying at anchor and resting from their lough cruises, had their masts and rails lined with smug, feathered stowaways, yellow bills resting on white puffed-out breasts. My eyes caught sight of a strong and powerful trace horse, bedecked with brasses, coming over the hump of the bridge, nostrils dilated as it strained to negotiate the treacherous incline. A coal bag tilted slightly on the cart, spilling some black shining nuggets onto the road.

It was now nearing 8.00 a.m. so, quickening my pace, I cut through Prince's Street – a street that could never be described as having a princely appearance, and by reputation must surely have been named after the Prince of Darkness. Swiftly I pressed on towards the Albert Clock, which I assumed, being poor at history, must have been designed by the same architect responsible for the Tower of Pisa. The consort stood loftily, scanning High Street from his alcove, a pigeon on his head, and with clear evidence that he had had many previous such feathered guests. Across I went towards Spackman's, where 'lads', we were led to believe, 'went with their dads to be clad'. In Corporation Street a flight of butterflies fluttered in my solar plexus region, and there it was – a large gloomy Victorian building, but to me the Palace of Oz. High above the roof, on spindly metal legs, was a massive square water tank emblazoned with the magic name, S.C. Allen.

The administrative offices were at one end of the building and at the other was a large loading bay. Beside the bay was my gateway to a professional future, an entrance to the world of opportunity and the possible fulfilment of a life's ambition. Not a monastery, by any means, no silence here, nor the gentle chant of a litany: the noise on entering was ear-shattering. I hesitated, as on stage, to consider an entrance. I mooched in.

The timekeeper was a smiling man with one arm. The other, I was told, had been lost at a guillotine, but despite this misfortune, he was happy. He looked up, bowed his head – not in reverence but in order to see the better over his spectacles – 'You're the new lad, aren't you?' he roared above the din. Having received a nodded affirmative, he bent over his book, marked the time, and jerked his head in the direction of a door, indicating that entrance had been granted.

Once through that door, I was paralysed by noise that made the assortment on the Queen's Bridge sound like Beethoven's Pastoral Symphony. I was confronted by large wooden troughs, about twelve feet by eight feet, which moved rhythmically backwards, forwards and sideways. A thousand glass marbles in sand and water were spun hither and thither on a zinc plate inside the trough. This was the process where plates were surfaced and prepared for the litho artist's hand. The noise created was shattering to the nervous system and the ears were none too pleased either.

I beat a hasty retreat up the wide and well-worn wooden stairway to the next floor and the compositors' room, where men set type for letterpress printing. The acrid fumes of melting lead assailed my nostrils, catching the back of my throat. A man sat at a Linotype machine, a typesetting monster that cut lines of type from brass dies. The operator sat at a keyboard, like a typist, or perhaps more closely resembling the Phantom of the Opera, shrouded as he was in a constant haze of blue fumes. It looked, and no doubt was, most unhealthy.

The next floor, in contrast, was peaceful. All that could be heard was the flutter and movement of paper, the happy chatter of female voices, and perhaps the gentle humming of a popular tune. It was the folding room, where the women neatly packed the posters. I had come from hell up to heaven. The top floor was the real heaven (or so I imagined), for that was where the artists' room was situated.

The first day at work is the longest day in one's life. An 8.10 a.m. start, one hour for lunch (and you do not leave the building), then a year-long afternoon that finishes at 5.50 p.m. After the short school day with all your pals for company, mickey-taking, fun and rough-and-tumble, you suddenly find yourself physically and mentally chained to a small desk in the corner of a very large room full of grim grown-ups. This room was glass-roofed and furnished with two long rows of benches, twenty-four in all. Each bench was heavy, like a butcher's table, measuring about

Working at Allen's with the lithographers (I'm third from right)

six and a half feet by five feet and bearing a lithographic silver-grey plate. Over each, overalled men bent, laboriously reproducing a separation colour for some poster or other. They did not look at all like the artists you expected to see; they were more like grocers in brown coats doing their accounts. This was hardly surprising – they were lithographers, just tradesmen doing an honest day's toil.

Allen's was, without any doubt, a superb training ground for any young aspiring artist. The early start activated the mind to the hardships a working man had to endure. The pay of six shillings and sixpence a week impressed upon you how long it would take to become filthy rich. It also helped you to realise the value your employer placed upon you. This valuation had the effect of modifying drastically any ideas you might have had of being especially talented. An early awareness that Allen's powers that be cared as much about you as they did about pit ponies was established. Thus it became obvious that you would have to use your own ingenuity to modify the system and so preserve your proper pride. Ingenious ploys would have to be adopted to ease your lot by avoiding those tasks that were demeaning, insulting and detestable

79

to a young man looking towards a bright horizon. The most baneful of these tasks were making ink and cleaning shading mediums, tasks that were the scourge of an apprentice's existence.

Inspiration is a blessing to be nurtured. It comes in many forms and, every so often, at very convenient times. It was during my third month in Allen's that the inspiration came to me that I should cultivate a little humility and that this might take me far on the road to liberty. I decided to demote myself to the role of errand boy. 'Do you need anything outside?' became my catch phrase, as I paraded round the artists' benches, notebook in hand. I was terribly willing and most able to get them anything they wanted outside the building. My expertise became such that I was able to talk some of them into sending for things they thought they needed. When I would hit the fresh air – and in those days it was appreciably fresher than now – with my notebook in hand, I used to think how appropriate was the name 'journeyman'. They could send me on as many journeys as they pleased. It was all so worth while when I thought about what I was avoiding. A little humility took me a long way.

Let me tell something of the two tasks I often succeeded in avoiding. First, the shading mediums, used for creating tints. They were in the form of wooden frames covered with a gelatinous textured material, with different textures available – linear, dotted, crosshatched, herringbone – multifarious patterns *ad nauseam*. In order to use this system of shading, the lithographer would cover his plate or stone with paper, leaving bare the area he wished to tint. In one corner of the artists' room sat a large litho stone covered with a gooey black ink rather like a thick sticky boot polish. With the stone was a roller or squeegee, and a few vigorous rolls of the squeegee gave it an even coverage of ink. This was then carefully transferred to the shading medium. Placing the medium over the exposed working area, the lithographer would then gently rub the back of the frame, thus transferring the chosen tint onto his plate. These shading mediums were indispensable to litho artists, particularly to those who were chromo workers, that is, the few men who worked on stone and reproduced small items such as labels and show cards. In Allen's these men were looked upon as superior beings, but apart from the fact that they did smaller-scale work, I saw nothing that justified this particular class demarcation. The dictionary says that chromolithography is a process of lithographing in colours. From this definition, all the lithographic artists were chromolithographers.

80

One of our chromo workers, a man with a face as long as a wet Sunday, belonged to a religious sect whose members can withdraw so far into themselves that they seem already to be in the next world. This particular gentleman could be seen in silent prayer before he started his work and again after he had finished. He created his own social cell and, monk-like, he would work within it in silence with the help of his saviour and a jeweller's eyeglass. It was understood that he disapproved of everyone and everything in his vicinity, especially apprentices. Such an attitude can, of course, work both ways. His fervent prayers were matched only by his religious devotion to the shading mediums. As we apprentices had to clean up after him, he was not number one on our popularity charts. When the working day came to an end, a demoralising number of black sticky mediums would have accumulated from him and other lithographers, and these, along with the stone and the roller, would have to be cleaned using rags, turpentine and a great deal of self-control. My friend Taylor Carson, with whom I escaped from the litho room a couple of times a week to attend classes at the Belfast College of Art, always presented a very strong case for his non-participation in this particular chore. He would use a plaintive voice, display a pair of dry and hacked hands and tell you he was allergic to turpentine. I was not allergic to the turpentine – I was allergic to the task. However, I persevered until the arrival of another apprentice to whom I gave a crash course. I then told him he had a natural aptitude for the work, that he did it much better than I did, and duly elected him Medium Control.

The making of ink was another onerous and detestable imposition. This task, Carson was not quite so adept at sidestepping. On many occasions I was able to bring the message-boy role into play and left him to boil along with the ink. What made this particular duty so obnoxious was first, the environment, and second, the air pollution.

Off the main artists' room were the bogs or, in more civilised parlance, the lavatory. This you entered through an antiquated green door knobbled with the paint runs of decades. Four rickety wooden steps led down into the L-shaped, evil-smelling grotto. It appeared that the cleaners, if ever there were any, had abdicated about the beginning of the twentieth century. Dickensian? It would have made Fagin's den look like a dentist's waiting room. The upstroke of the L housed the lavatory, which was surely the prototype of the original flusher. The horizontal stroke of the L boasted a large and very grubby sink or jaw

box. Coloured yellow-ochre on the outside, the monstrosity was very chipped and the chips were ingrained with the mire of decades. Two skinny, desolate taps, like noses dripping perpetually into the filthy basin, could have proudly claimed to be solid brass had anyone cared enough to tackle the years of grime that encrusted them. An ancient black slotted draining board to the left of the sink seemed to drink more than it drained, thus acquiring the blackness of ebony. To the right of the sink a medieval gas ring nestled in a bed of greasy black spillage, a legacy from years of ink-making. The area was lit by one indecently naked light bulb which gave forth a dim pulsating yellow glow – probably another prototype, this time from Mr Edison. Add to this comparatively modern lighting system a pathetic, feeble glimmer of daylight, straining desperately to penetrate the heavy layer of dust and dirt on a tiny window, and you have the stage set. To say the air was thick is to be polite; mixed with lavatorial aromas and the stench of boiling litho crayons, the air (if that is the right word) could have burst into flames or exploded.

In this environment the apprentice stood over the hot gas ring, stirring his pot of melting litho chalk stubs, adding water and involuntarily inhaling the strong fumes as he made the ink. Such recycling is for me a thing of the past. Thank God – I have lived through it.

Another slavish hardship was to be confined in a darkroom where a photographic slide of the poster design was projected onto inch-squared paper, each sheet being sixty inches by forty inches. A sixteen-sheet poster would consist of four such sheets. There were also thirty-two-sheet, forty-eight-sheet and sixty-four-sheet posters. Naturally enough, the length of your term in 'solitary' was determined by the size of your poster. When the design was projected to the required size, we apprentices would outline the image with conté-crayon. Each area of colour was carefully traced, and where a highlight occurred we would let X mark the spot. Corner marks were indicated most accurately, as it was on these that colour registration depended. Once completed, the tracing would be transferred to litho plates, and drawn in ink by the lithographer to create a key drawing for the work. From this, master plates would be prepared, using a red ochre keel powder which, being nongreasy, would give the guidelines without itself appearing in the final production.

Placing a sheet of paper on the plate to avoid the transference of grease from his hand to its surface, the artist would settle down to the task ahead. With the original design before him, the lithographer would study it carefully, analysing what colour had been delegated to him. With his crayon and ink he would work on that single colour. Posters were always drawn and printed lightest colours first; this required great skill in order to gauge the varying intensities of one colour and how it would stand up to over-printing. It also required a good eye, extreme confidence, a sure hand, and a strong colour sense to be an expert lithographer. Allen's had experts in abundance and through them a fine reputation was built.

It was an impressive sight to see the long lines of giant printing machines churning out famous posters, the feeders (the women who stood on high platforms at the printing presses) leafing the sheets into the hungry monsters, the blue-overalled printers fussing around, checking and rechecking progress, then rushing to mix furiously at the inks they spread on the rollers, keeping those voracious appetites satisfied. From those machines poured some of the finest printing in the British Isles, with orders coming from the biggest trade names in commerce. The Guinness advertising was always my favourite and to this day still maintains a frontrunner position. Possibly the most unpopular poster we printed – though without doubt the most historic – was one for recruitment to Sir Oswald Mosley's British Union of Fascists.

Although I enjoyed the feeling of being a member of the setup at Allen's, and I really appreciated the training I was privileged to receive,

I could never claim to be happy as an employee. The artists' room, with all the men working slavishly over their litho plates, had as much art about it atmospherically as the machine shop in a foundry. With the exception of three men, none of the lithographers had an interest in painting or drawing. They were tradesmen, accomplished at what they were trained to do, nothing more, nothing less.

The large artists' room housed a glass-paned office which took up about one-seventh of the floor space. In this office the staff handled all records in connection with the art department. A small section at the end of this built-in greenhouse was the office of the foreman, H. Echlin Neill. Being the foreman had its drawbacks in the popularity polls. Always a kind and helpful man, he was a superb lithographer, and a very talented painter, gifts that added to his unpopularity in that factory atmosphere. His authority over the brown-coated lithographic crew was about as effective as Captain Bligh's over the *Bounty* when he was in the longboat.

A catastrophe struck the department when Echlin had to step down as foreman for some reason known only to management. He was replaced by a very tall gentleman from that place people irritatingly refer to as 'the mainland'. He looked like an ex-soldier, and his long face and languid walk created an instant impression on the lithographers. The impression was such that he lasted only a short time, and Echlin was reinstated. However, management was still unhappy and soon poor Echlin was again dethroned, to be replaced by yet another Englishman. Fred Dawe came with splendid references as an extremely competent commercial artist who did work for the most prestigious firms. He was a bespectacled and handsome widower, and a gentleman he was in the true sense of the word. His hair was silver, well smoothed back with a side parting, not a strand awry, and a small matching moustache nestled under an aquiline nose. Impeccably dressed in black jacket and striped trousers, his elegance was highlighted by the backdrop of brown-overalled litho men. He was the cartoonist's standard image of the London businessman. He was not just a pretty face, either, as he proved by creating some stunning showcard designs on his arrival and before taking command. His son, of whom he was extremely fond, was Cedric Dawe, then one of the leading British scenic designers on films, responsible for the sets in countless major productions.

In the office at this time worked a pretty young woman called Anna

Faulkner. Anna was to fall under the spell of Fred Dawe's charm to such an extent that they became husband and wife. This automatically made Fred brother-in-law to Brian Faulkner, who was later to become prime minister of Northern Ireland.

When S.C. Allen's went into voluntary liquidation in 1940, Taylor Carson and myself were offered scholarships to the art college by its principal, Ivor Beaumont. We grabbed the opportunity with four hands, because this meant, instead of being released for two days a week, we would now be full-time students.

Courtesy of Guinness
Museum, Dublin

11

THE SCHOOL OF LIFE

THE BELFAST COLLEGE OF ART was, to me, heaven on earth. Taylor Carson was as keen as myself and, like me, he could not get enough of the excellent tuition available. I enjoyed the college so much that I did a couple of extra years there. At the same time I was drawing for magazines like *London Opinion*. I could not have the same studio facilities at home, because Mother, being of a Victorian mould, would never have condoned me having a nude model in the drawing room – particularly one as attractive as the model we had in the life class. A mother who did her utmost to keep her sons to herself never approved if a designing female hove in sight, and in her mind all females were designers. However, the threat of life-drawing in the sanctity of her home never arose. The college had too big a hold on me and no small part of that was the bevy of attractive female designers.

The art college in those days occupied the top floor of the Belfast College of Technology, that green-domed mass of indeterminate architecture that successfully masks half the Georgian dignity of the Royal Belfast Academical Institution – a major blunder by city planners. As you entered the hallowed portals, to the right was an aperture in the wall from whence an inquisitive face would peer. This was where you purchased your requirements for the day ahead – large sheets of cartridge paper for a penny, pencils, rubbers, anything you needed, at prices which, when you look back, seem untrue. Now we have indifferent sketch pads costing pounds, pencils about eight times more expensive and rubbers mostly made of plastic. Having collected the essentials from the aforementioned aperture, the fittest of us would race up the stone stairway to the top floor. The less fit, or even downright lazy, would head for the lift. There were often mad impulses to race the lift to the

9.15½ A.M.

"WOT TIME IS THIS TO COME IN AT?"
Ivor Beaumont

86

Left to right: myself, Barney Doherty and Taylor Carson

top, a feat which was accomplished quite regularly without any losses, other than that of breath.

Ivor Beaumont was a small man with bushy eyebrows which met in a perpetual frown over his nose, the bridge adorned with some hairs. He had the sharp eyes of an owl, and his beaked nose, which shaded a tight mouth and a slightly jutted, but rounded chin, made him resemble even more closely that bird of the night. His grey hair, which had no great attention lavished on what there was of it, projected at the sides, classifying him as one of the long-eared variety of owl. His temper was not on a long fuse.

Newton Penprase, a Cornish man and lecturer supreme, was equally small, and what hair he had looked like a grey laurel wreath around a parchment-coloured pate. He too had bushy eyebrows, shading sharp blue, but kindly, eyes. He hummed to himself as he skimmed along the corridors. Although he usually appeared to be of a most happy disposition, he could erupt like a volcano without warning. Fortunately, it never happened with his students, but quite often with his sparring partner, Mr Beaumont. An antipathy existed between the two that often resulted in battles royal. Loud, even hair-raising, noises would issue from the headmaster's office, echoing and re-echoing round the hard marble-floored corridors. Students and lecturers would get offside and feign deafness. When the protagonists eventually put in appearances at their

87

various classes, the scars of battle, although obvious, would go unnoticed by everyone. Familiarity had bred consent.

Our anatomy teacher was Seamus Stoupe, then an ageing old codger, kind and gentle, and in accord with his name he had the stoop of age. His ruddy and lined angular face was like a farmer's, well and truly weathered, though it is possible that much of his colour might have been helped by the barley crop. I did two years with him, and he was a good man with whom to study anatomy.

Bill Murray

Poster design, in the hands of Scotsman Bill Murray, was more or less a waste of time for both Taylor Carson and myself, as we were both deeper into that subject than the teacher. But he was good for chat and funny stories. A big blustering man with black brilliantined hair, powerfully built, immaculately dressed, and with a nose that looked as if it had been in a boxing ring or a rugby tackle, Bill was a very distinctive figure as he stormed along the corridors with a large pipe held tightly in an even larger mouth of strong white teeth. That perpetual grin of the pipe smoker, dictated by his dentured grip on the pipe, was stamped on his face, and a series of blue Indian smoke signals trailed in his wake.

The life class was in the capable hands of a Mr Mansfield, who was about five feet ten and of a strong build. His brown hair stood up in a quiff above his tall forehead, and his dark eyebrows were perpetually raised over glasses that rested precariously and somewhat crookedly on a largish aquiline nose, which he held rather snootily in a skyward direction. He was given to collision courses, often bumping into desks and chairs, or tripping on unseen objects – all caused, no doubt, by the proud angle of his proboscis. His most common expression was 'Oh, de-ah', which was hardly surprising, considering his aptitude for finding obstacles. He had a large head on a very long neck which sported a generous Adam's apple. Long of body and short of leg, he was one of the most caricaturable of lecturers. From the back of his head to his heels you could have drawn a straight line.

"HELLEW FRIAS"

Mr Mansfield

At the age of fourteen I had crashed into our unlocked bathroom, and there in the bath of bubbles was the tanned and very shapely body of an American cousin who was staying with us at the time. I stood frozen to the spot and spluttered apologies as my young eyes slithered over the gleaming wet body.

Brother Ian's voice roared upstairs from behind me, 'Don't stand there apologising all evening. Close the door and get out of there.'

That was my first sight of a woman's naked body – or rather, the upper part of it. It was when I entered Mansfield's life class that I had the full baptism. I received the 'full body' blow. In class you sat on one chair with your drawing board resting on the back of the chair in front. The model, a pretty redhead, stood in a conventional pose, and as the full impact of her nakedness swamped me, I felt the blush radiate from my face. I slowly raised my board and slumped further down in my chair. This exercise enabled me to cover her body completely and just leave in vision the head, which I drew in fine detail. As I drew, with legs crossed and the board resting on my knees, my left foot, which was taking the weight, started to vibrate. This resulted in my drawing board taking up the rhythm and tapping out a tattoo on the chair back. I felt all the eyes of the class were upon me and I truly believe I have never been more embarrassed in my life. Mansfield soon made me overcome my inhibitions and before long I managed the full form. I did not ever become one of that lecturer's favourite students, because I could never appreciate his particular approach to figure drawing. Penprase was the big influence when my style was being formed, and his technique was worlds apart from Mansfield's.

Antique form – drawing from statues – was the lot of one Sam Taylor, a dour and most serious man, well loved by Taylor Carson and the painter Maurice Wilks. Sadly, I was not his most popular student, either. He always seemed to get more dour and a lot more serious when I

entered the antiques room. I had a strong suspicion that he had some objection to my throwing my hat onto the head of *The Discus Thrower*, and hanging my coat over the athlete's extended arm. I was never invited to his house, as were the others, but that was possibly good thinking on his part. The antique figure class was about the only one I did not enjoy; I felt it had the atmosphere of a graveyard.

We had in the college a rare character, Fred Allen, son of a north-country coal miner. Fred, so he told me, had also worked in the mines himself. I cannot recall what we did in his class, apart from learning to say 'damn' in his dialect, and also 'bloody' as a bonus. He wrote art critiques for the *Belfast News-Letter* for years and ended up teaching in Methodist College. I can remember his dark sleek hair and heavy-lidded dark eyes, sallow complexion, slightly hollowed temples in a high brow, and his prominent cheekbones with concave cheeks. Gaunt of appearance, but fun to be with, he was very much one of the boys rather than a lecturer. The friendly approach worked wonders for Fred, and though I find it hard to recall what we were supposed to be doing in that class, we really did one helluva lot and learned more than existed on the curriculum. Good fellowship, confidence and relaxation were some of the additions to damn and bloody.

One day he approached me in class with a very mischievous gleam in his dark eyes. I wondered what was to follow, but you could never read his mind – he was never obvious.

'Friers,' he said, 'I'm challenging you to a duel.'

I thought it must be 4B pencils at four pages and I had guessed right.

'I will draw a funny drawing with my right hand and you will do one with your left. Let's see who is the better man,' he announced.

Gerry Dillon looked up from his easel, where he was surrounded by dozens of discarded attempts at a still life. Like myself, he wondered at the challenge, and maybe he was even interested in the outcome. Fred Allen was left-handed, and his mind thought that this morning was a good one for crazy experiments. I accepted the challenge without forewarning him that I could, albeit slowly, draw with my left.

The papers were set up and Fred took his position. He, like many left-handers, had a most awkward-looking approach, his elbow pointing straight out in front of him and his left hand bent at the wrist. He looked as though his arm had been broken at the shoulder and his wrist had not come off too well either. On this occasion he looked even more

90

awkward than normal. We started to draw and after only a few lines the famous 'damn' rang out and he declared it no contest. I remained silent about being ambidextrous, as I could not remember the word at the time.

Gerry Dillon pinned up his twenty-second sheet and launched into another bowl of fruit. He used to say the thing he hated most was 'Friers laughing at his paintings'. He got that all wrong. I laughed, not at his paintings, but at the fact that he did so many in a session. By the time the rest of the class had finished painting that bowl of fruit, many sessions would have passed, and, the fruit having dried up, we would be drawing on our memories. Gerry seemed to draw on impulse, as he had barely looked at the subject for more than a few minutes before an impression fluttered down to join the pile at his feet.

For modelling and sculpture we had the inimitable and incredible George McCann. His appearances in class for actual tuition were brief, to put it mildly. When he did deign to extend a stay, it was to talk about his adventures as an officer in the army, about India and life with the Inniskillings or, most likely, to explain how he had not been paid and could he borrow a few bob. Like Billy Bunter or Micawber, he was always expecting something to turn up, in the form of cash, to relieve his embarrassing predicament. My late friend Barney Doherty, who was always more burdened with, than short of, cash, was an obvious target for George to home in on. Barney, being a generous soul, never, ever minded. Money meant nothing to him and he liked old George, as did we all. Like my dear friend, money meant nothing to me either, as I never had any. On any occasion when I might have had a few bob to rattle together, I made sure they did not rattle within earshot of George.

McCann was to be replaced by a Scottish lecturer called John Knox, who arrived one day and, extending his hand to George, announced, 'I am John Knox.' George, who was never short of a caustic reply, answered, 'That's a coincidence, I'm John Wesley.' That was how the story went and although probably apocryphal, it was certainly characteristic. George was married to the one and only Mercy Hunter and was therefore brother-in-law to the chief inspector of art for schools, Colonel John Hunter. They completed a formidable trio of art teachers.

Many stories were told, and still circulate, of George's exploits. He was a great friend to many people, the well-to-do and the ne'er-do-well, the famous and the infamous. Well in with the literary set, he was a very close friend of W.R. Rodgers and Louis MacNeice. One macabre tale about George, be it fact or fable, concerns the demise of Louis MacNeice, and is too good to be ignored. Louis, it was said, died somewhere in Wales, and George, his closest of friends, was delegated to collect the great man's ashes and return them to the land of saints and scholars. This duty George willingly undertook. Following the funeral service, the usual heads got together to chat, over a jar or two, about the dear departed. Eventually, with a plane to catch, George dragged himself from the wake. It can be assumed that he may have dozed a bit on the plane, as many of us are wont to do. He disembarked at Nutt's Corner, feeling as one would feel following such a trip. Halfway across the tarmac he made the discovery that he was unaccompanied. 'Good God, where's Louis?' he roared – and George could project. 'Where has the old so-and-so got to?'

People started to take an interest as George hurried back towards the plane, pushing through the oncoming passengers, all the time shouting for Louis. Requests about what he looked like, his height, and where he had been sitting, were ignored, as the desperate but determined figure of George ploughed on. Needless to say, no one had the slightest clue as to where Louis was, and the plane search was abandoned. It seems, so the story goes, that Louis was found, still sitting on a bar counter in Wales, a day later. Many are the tales of George, but that is a biography for someone else's pen.

Although each and every one of the art lecturers contributed something to my future career, there was only one, as is often the case, who was the real moulder of thought. This opinion I hold would, I know, be confirmed by my longtime friend and fellow artist, Raymond Piper. The natural forms class, where you drew or painted plants, flowers, birds and animals, consisted of two students – Raymond and myself. The lecturer was Newton Penprase, and we had the great good fortune to have the full benefit of his outstanding abilities as a teacher. It was he who made us aware of the range of colour you could get with a pencil alone, colour created by sensitivity of touch, a delicate line drawn with minimum pressure for where the light was hitting your object, then the pressure increasing for the areas in shade. A flower would be drawn in line only, yet it could have dimension, light and shade. Pen had that knack of making you think with the pencil, so much

9·15 A.M.

"MORNING DEAR"!

Newton Penprase

92

so that your fingers became as deft as those of a flute player.

To draw a bird or an animal, he would not permit you to rough the subject out beforehand. 'No, boy,' he would say, 'study the form, keep it locked in your mind. Then start from its eye, tail, or wherever you please, drawing it hair by hair, or feather by feather. You have a sure line, so draw without hesitation, keeping the whole shape in mind, and though you may, in the first few attempts, go a little awry, you will master it in no time, I assure you.'

At that time it seemed all wrong, because we had roughed everything out in other classes. However, he proved to be right, and for both Piper and myself he created a confidence in approach that has proved invaluable. I can start at an eye or an ear and complete the subject without that jumble of lines that go to making a layout. Raymond, too, is very positive, and his draughtsmanship can never be denied.

To emphasise Penprase's interest in his charges, I must relate one very characteristic instance. I had just completed a drawing of a kestrel and was doodling on one corner of my sheet, trying to dream up a cartoon. Penprase entered the room at his usual high rate of knots.

'Well, boy, how are we getting on?' He scanned the kestrel. 'Um, very good, boy, very good,' he commented.

Then his eye caught the cartoon. He sniffed, and left the room even faster than he had entered. He was hardly out of the door before he appeared again. A plaster hand was thrown onto my board. I looked up at him with what must surely have been an enquiring expression.

'Go ahead, boy – study it carefully and draw it.'

'Yes, sir', was the wondering answer.

'Remember, boy, when you do those funny drawings of yours, you don't just draw hands like a bunch of bananas. Hands can express as much as the face. An actor who cannot use his hands is only half an actor. Always remember when you are drawing your cartoons, or doing a painting involving the human, that hands are vitally important and can add much to making that work live.'

There ended a lesson that was never forgotten.

Pen took a modelling class during a period when I was to enter the Ballsbridge Competition in Dublin. One of my entries was to be a portrait head. Perfectionist that he was, Pen made me model a skull first and over that I had to build the portrait. I won that Ballsbridge Prize, thanks to Newton Penprase and his method of teaching.

12

WAR COMES TO BELFAST

M Y BROTHER IAN, who in his early years emulated the great screen lover Rudolph Valentino, had his hair so well plastered down that it looked like tar side-parted. With a Nöel-Coward-style cigarette holder and dressed to kill, he must have run the screen heart-throb very close in the number of his conquests. His tonsorial titivating was no doubt responsible for his parting increasing in width to such a degree that it was all parted before he was thirty. Though he may have wished to look like Valentino, he actually resembled Franchot Tone. A very talented artist and a superb draughtsman, he only drew to amuse himself, possibly put off by Mother's advice to 'look for a good steady job like the customs and excise or the civil service'. What fascination the customs and excise had for Mother, I never knew.

Through her guidance Ian became a law clerk with the firm of C. and J. Black. He was with them for a long period before he broke with the law to seek something new, and there followed a period as manager of Councillor T.L. Cole's estates. I believe – or at least I was told by Ian – that when council elections were coming up, the councillor's slogan was 'Cole is not slack'. Tiring rapidly of that occupation, Ian was encouraged by Cambridge's husband, Fraser Mayne, to join the staff of W. Erskine Mayne. This was a period when Erskine Mayne's was one of Belfast's big family businesses. Ian spent most of his time in their radio, and later television, shop, pouring all his artistic talents into window displays. When war clouds loomed over Europe and his country needed him more desperately than Erskine Mayne's, he answered the call.

Our shop in the Lagan Village was sold in 1939 and we moved to

IAN 1949

My brother Ian, 1949
(Photograph by Studio
Gay Warren)

Dundonald. The horse-drawn maroon-coloured *Belfast Telegraph* delivery vans were getting more and more active as the war came closer. Special editions seemed to be coming out hourly and the billboards on the back of the vans became more alarming. Possibly the funniest bill head in that time of tension was the announcement: CRISIS GETTING WORSE. Not the reaction of an over-anxious editor, but definitely a concise summation of the view of the man in the pub.

To talk of war years is to talk of your whole lifetime. I do not remember a year when there was not a war going on somewhere or

other. Memories are short where mayhem is concerned. We do have
cenotaphs and we do have a Remembrance Day, a couple of minutes'
silence, but we can, and do, forget the fallen until the following year.
The Second World War was the big one, where names were made.
Monty, Alexander, Brooke, Eisenhower, MacArthur et cetera, et cetera;
other names, in their hundreds of thousands, were carved in stone.
Hitler sent his robotic masses jackbooting where he willed. He gave Mr
Chamberlain that beaten docket, and the British were shouldering what
arms they had against the massed maniacs of der Führer.

MACKIE'S MAGAZIN

VOLUME 2 No 14   DECEMBER. 1

CHRISTMAS WAR EDITIO

Coming home from S.C. Allen's, my eye was drawn to a news ven-
dor's poster, on which it said: 'First bombs of war dropped on *Iron
Duke*'. A cold sweat broke on my brow, because now I felt we really
were in the war. Ian was on the *Iron Duke*, his first posting in the Royal
Navy Volunteer Reserve. My mind could only absorb the worst. I could
imagine the *Iron Duke* as a tangled mass of metal. Like HMS *Caroline*, the
Iron Duke had long since come out of active service, and its main purpose was to serve as headquarters for the admiral of Shetland and the
Orkneys.

Ian, thank God, was not to suffer anything more serious than a cold
plunge in Scapa Flow. A few days after the bombing, he sent his gold
watch home with the explanation that he had gone in for a swim and
overlooked removing his timepiece before the plunge. His story of the
bombing was funny. Apparently, a couple of Norwegian-based German
Stukas dropped from the skies, releasing their deadly missiles on the antique warship, believing it to be a potential threat to the Third Reich.
Crew members of the *Duke*, in chain formation, were handing shells up
to the gunners from the arsenal. Unfortunately, the gunners had taken
to the briny. Once this fact had sunk in, the unanimous decision to
abandon ship was enthusiastically adopted. Ian, though a strong swimmer, was also not one to take any chances. He pounced on a float – one
of those large wooden affairs that resemble waffle irons – and pushed it
overboard. He hurriedly gathered whatever possessions he wished to
save, and returned to the side of the ship to take his leave. When he
looked over to where he had dropped the float, he saw a solid square
of naval types waist-deep in water, but afloat – on his float. He jumped
overboard, swam round for a while, and was picked up by a fishing boat.
Later, when the gunners were questioned about their sudden departure,
their defence was that they had no defence. To put it another way, the

guns were out of date and could not be angled far enough or fast enough to be of use. Also, they added sardonically, 'It would take too long for the fuses to burn down.'

A few days after the *Iron Duke* attack, Ian was walking on the island when another Nazi plane decided to give him a burst of machine-gun fire. He leaped into some bushes and escaped unscathed. It makes you wonder, did the Nazis reckon him to be a key figure in the war, prompting them to send out a Red Baron to get him? *C'est la guerre*. Hitler seemed determined to get Ian. It was, or appeared to be, a personal vendetta masterminded by Adolph. Everywhere Ian was posted, he seemed to attract the bombers. He was stationed in London during some of the worst raids; they sought him out in Portsmouth and everywhere else the admiralty tried to hide him; he even came home on leave to experience the blitzes Belfast endured. Had he been able to face the sea, he could not have suffered many more close encounters. He was a volunteer many years prior to the outbreak of war, and I often wondered why he ever joined. He was, indeed, a very strong swimmer, and he loved the sea. When we took family trips to Bangor, Ian would swim the whole length of Ballyholme Bay and back. That was his routine, no messing around, just a long swim and a swift towelling. However, much as he loved the sea in that sense, he dreaded the thought of sailing. The question – Why join the RNVR? – begs an answer. That answer is simple. The holidays were good – Bournemouth, Torquay, Isle of Wight, Portsmouth, and all on board ships at anchor. For Ian, the hardest part of war was coming home on leave. He would be wearing his full kit, including a heavy duffel coat, and thus clad, whatever the conditions, would be hanging over the rails of the Liverpool boat, nigh unto death. Fellow passengers would be sympathetic with him, in the belief that he must surely be suffering the traumas of a recent Murmansk convoy.

Those war years were grim, hard, tragic, terrifying, and exciting. When the news came through of battles lost, everyone was in the doldrums. William Joyce, Lord Haw-Haw, would be in his sneering element, and people were known to smash their radios in frustration at that drawling voice enumerating Allied setbacks and the glorious victories of Hitler's panzer divisions. *Deutschland über Alles*. Churchill was defiant and ready to fight in back entries if necessary. The RAF, a mere handful, was taking to the air and teaching the mighty Luftwaffe how to nose-dive. Bluebirds were to be over the white cliffs of Dover, and doodle

Wednesday 16 April 1941: a scene of destruction on the corner of Hillman Street and the Antrim Road (Courtesy of PRONI)

bugs and V2 rockets were over everywhere. We had utility labels and evacuee labels, ration books, dried milk, dried eggs, and dried potatoes. All the Allied national anthems were played before the radio news, a policy that got a little wearing after a time. Some of the anthems sounded like records played at the wrong speed.

The first air raid on Belfast, 7–8 April 1941, had little or no great effect on us at Dundonald. I was in bed and I must have been wakened by the anti-aircraft guns at a battery close to Dundonald cemetery. I recall sitting up in bed and calling my brother Bill, who was a bit irritated at being roused. 'Look, there seems to be a fire in town,' I said, pointing to a pulsating glow on the immediate horizon. Then came the flying onions: these anti-aircraft shells were shot with such rapidity that they looked like strings of onions. The distant command – 'Fi-ah!' – followed by wompha, wompha, wompha, as upwards through the probing searchlight beams crisscrossing the black velvet sky they soared, bright orange, until finally exploding into blue-white star bursts. Flak, flak, flak, just like a giant fireworks display and no more startling until you heard the distinctive and ominous whine of German bombs hurtling earthwards.

The second air raid on Belfast a week later was nightmarish. The sirens had barely finished their doleful moan when Keelong, our house, was invaded by cousins, aunts, nephew and niece from Belfast, all seeking sanctuary in rural Dundonald. All who could piled in under the stairs, while the others sought shelter under tables. The moon hung in an indigo sky and the stillness of the night, following the air-raid warning, was broken by the sinister pulsating drone of German bombers. Anti-aircraft guns hiccuped into life, perforating the sky with fairy lights of death. Then suddenly it was daylight. The whole landscape for miles around sat out in bold relief. I remember Cambridge saying, 'How clever, to light the sky in order to see the planes.' However, as the flares floated earthwards, it became all too evident that the advantage was to the high-flying Heinkels. You could have read a newspaper in the road, if you were brave enough, or mad enough, to venture out there. All hell broke loose, anti-aircraft fire mingling with the shrieks of falling bombs. A long night of terror began, and to those of us crushed under the stairs and tables, it seemed like an eternity. A stick of bombs fell on Dundonald, killing one man. The noise of that deluge of death, and the sight of Belfast ablaze, are a horrendous memory.

Some days later, when I went into town with Bill, the abomination of war was really driven home. The appalling destruction of property, the stench of burning in the air, and the huge holes in the roads left by bombs, impressed upon me the wickedness of mankind. The most horrendous sight of all was to see St George's Market filled with the white-sheeted bodies of the dead, countless lines of innocent citizens who had failed to survive the horror of that night. The public baths on the Falls Road housed the mangled bodies of other victims. It was a night when

Donegall Place, July 1941; vacant ground where Brands department store had previously stood (Courtesy of PRONI)

99

the evil of Nazi Germany chose Belfast as its victim, a night when families were blown to eternity, countless maimed, and the nation left to mourn 'man's inhumanity to man'.

Out of the tragedy and darkness of the war years there were always occasions when optimism rose up and your sanity was preserved. From turmoil rose creativity in our family circle, when Ian started to send home sketches of ideas he had had for using natural wood shapes to make animals and birds. On his return he got to work creating wildlife forms, utilising the eccentricities of branch shapes, the bark and natural grains, to achieve the textures of his subject. From these whimsies (his own description) he advanced to wood sculpture, and produced most superb and original works of art. He exhibited in Dublin and in the Royal Ulster Academy, of which he was an academician. How proud

100

he would have been had he lived to see his son Julian become one of the best wildlife artists in Britain. There can be no doubt that his creative mind and undoubted talent must have strongly influenced his son.

They were a tired bunch of men, but very jolly, their begrimed faces wreathed in happy smiles. Theirs was the happiness of men who had done a job well. Caps at jaunty angles, the collars of their heavy leather jackets pulled up around their ears, they dumped their bags at the hotel reception desk. The leather jackets bore the heavy, almost garish, emblems of the US army. These were some of the heroes of the Second World War, men who did a really tough, boring, and most essential job: they were ferry pilots. Because of their tough characters and perpetual optimism, a steady flow of bombers was delivered for the Allied offensives. They were gum-chewing, wisecracking guys who could well have walked off a film set.

The Union Hotel in Donegall Square South was the reception area for these boisterous crews. A hotel no more, it was now the American Officers' Club, and the duty officer at reception was myself. The GIs were a source of great inspiration to me, and this being so, I had managed to infiltrate to their very core. 'Hiya, Bud. Like some candy?' they would chorus, and before you could even mouth a reply, you would be showered with chocolate and candies, gum and cigarettes. They were most generous and they felt good when they were handing out gifts, particularly to a rationed people.

My function at reception was really to act as information officer. Most of the information was vital for military morale: 'Where could a guy meet a dame?'; or, 'Buddy, where's the nearest dance hall at?' Such information, though not classified, was undeniably specialised. While I was painting a mural in the club's billiard room, I met lots of people and made many friends. I met the world heavyweight boxing champion Joe Louis, who was then a top sergeant and aide. I had three particular friends at the club: two nurses, Lieutenants Carleston and Stone, and a naval officer, Lieutenant Commander Farrell. They were lots of fun, as Americans can be. Grace Stone presented me with a book, _Crescent Carnival_, by Frances Parkinson Keyes. A large romantic tome, it had a hero called Raoul. Apart from Grace thinking it was worth reading, it also had an obvious added attraction.

One great treat was given me by Farrell, and that was a visit to the ship on which he served. It was no ordinary visit, but an invitation to dinner. The ship was one of those churned out by Mr Kaiser in the US, called liberty ships, speedily built to increase Allied tonnage. They were no luxury liners. The dinner on board, at a period of ration cards and belt-tightening, was like a banquet at the Ritz: a six-course meal, with a thick steak, American apple pie, chocolate pudding, ice cream, side salads, white bread, brown bread, cakes, sugar, everything in plentiful supply – a most pleasant change from the home front's dehydrated delicacies.

Maybe it was because they were better fed that the Yanks seemed so different from our troops. They exuded good humour and a cavalier attitude to the situation. It could be that at that particular time they had not yet experienced the full force of war. Still, I do think we recognised their ability to raise people's spirits. Those expansive and flamboyant personalities did a lot for morale.

When they arrived in Northern Ireland they did not have to look too far for dames. Girls of all shapes and sizes launched a four-pronged attack on the GI Joes. A wild assortment of *femmes fatales* materialised, man-hungry, good-time gals. Pink fur-fabric short jackets, short skirts and high heels, bleached hair and faces made up like clowns betrayed the inexperienced. St-Trinian's-type schoolgirls were mixing with the more seasoned campaigners. Hank, Al and Elmer were no match for Lizzie, Maggie and Bessie, who were more of a menace than the 'snowballs' or shore patrols. The adventuresses clung to their Yanks like limpet mines. Many GIs were to fall in that battle of the sexes. 'A lat of themmuns said wur brogues wuz stickin' out': this, translated, simply meant the GIs were captivated by the northern dialects.

The Yanks could not have appreciated how much they owed to my youthful decadence, my sorties into the social sheughs of Northern Ireland. Your teenage years is the time when girls take on a new importance, the time when your masculine pride starts to battle with your shyness, the period when a very young man looks at very sophisticated screen lovers and wishes to emulate them, when he starts to shave from his chin that which a rough towel would remove, when his pulse and heartbeat get completely out of control should a pretty girl appear. This is the time when the easiest way to get a girl in your arms is to learn to dance. So it was with Taylor Carson and myself, we just had to go to dancing classes. Carson, being of a somewhat less retiring nature than

102

myself, led the way and we joined Sammy Leckey's Castle Dance Studio.

Situated in an entry off Castle Street, the dance studio could not, by any stretch of the imagination, inspire romantic thoughts. It was gloomy and barn-like, with chairs set around its dark walls. It could charitably be described as utilitarian. Mr Leckey, professional that he was, would patiently take us through the initial steps and even show us how to chassé. 'One-two, three chassé; one-two, three chassé.' After a few of these instructions on how to count up to three and chassé, which, though it sounds perfectly simple, could prove a very complicated exercise indeed to a footless over-sensitive young man like myself, Carson seemed to be taking to it like a duck to water, though it has to be admitted he had fewer inhibitions than I and, without doubt, showed a greater keenness to conquer all difficulties. When a record was put on and music blared forth, some lady instructors would appear from the gloom to 'lift' you. My first and lasting image of that class was that neither Terpsichore nor Aphrodite had seen fit to cast their spell upon me. Out of the gloom loomed to lift me a vision of such terrifying appearance that my hand shakes as I pen the very recollection. She had a short, exceedingly plump, figure encased in a short black dress that clung to her body like a wet bathing costume, revealing the tortuous contours of her figure. Her legs were strong and bandy, like a soccer player's. Black greasy hair framed the pale fat face and her mouth, which was large, was in perpetual motion as she chewed on her gum.

With hands on hips she looked at me contemptuously and said, 'Are ye gittin' up or sittin'?'

Against my will I got up, and she said, in the thinly disguised voice of a woman of little patience, 'You're supposed to lead aff.'

I noticed the black dress was heavily stained with grease around the ample bosom, a legacy, no doubt, of many fish-and-chip suppers. I led aff. There followed a disastrous display of ineptitude on my part and a crash course in obscenities from the woman in black as, to the music, I rhythmically crushed her feet.

Feeling convinced that I was endangering the woman's career, I shamefacedly proffered an apology. 'I can't dance,' I understated.

'Jazus! You're tellin' me,' she snapped.

It is funny how a little incident like that can take the edge off one's appetite. It was to be many years before I disgraced a dance floor again.

'Now the book said to put my LF forward in PP moving LOD diagonal to wall. RF forward. But... er... which is my LF?'

13

TAKING PEN TO PAPERS

WHILE IAN WAS CARRYING OUT vital wartime responsibilities drawing the enemy fire, I used to write to him regularly. These letters I would illustrate profusely, to bolster his morale. In one letter written in 1939 while I was still at Allen's, I enclosed a cartoon comment on the Russo-Finnish war, a strip cartoon depicting Stalin as a giant being outmanoeuvred in a hand-to-hand against a tiny Finnish giant killer. In the mess with Ian was a journalist who worked for the *Portsmouth Evening News*, and the cartoon was so much appreciated by the assembled mess that it ended up in that newspaper. That was my first professional cartoon, for which I received a half-guinea (ten shillings and sixpence, or fifty-two and a half pence), and I was firmly convinced that I was on the road to untold wealth. Understandable when you remember that Allen's paid six shillings and sixpence for a week's work.

After my cartoon was published in the Portsmouth paper, I started submitting work to *London Opinion, Reynolds' News, Punch, Courier,* and *Everybody's*. I also started to receive commissions to illustrate Northern Ireland programmes in the *Radio Times*. During the *London Opinion* association I was chosen, as one of a select few, to be written up by Percy V. Bradshaw in a series printed in the magazine. These articles appeared under the title 'They make us smile'. Bradshaw ran a correspondence art school, which had as its slogan 'Let me be your father'. I was quite pleased to be adopted by him when he started to write those pen portraits!

London Opinion, Tower House, Southampton Street, Strand, London, was the publication to give me a first contact with a real live editor, professionally speaking, and my first solo visit to London, specifically to meet a real live editor. Perhaps this description gives a somewhat

104

'THE McCOOEYS'

ARE BACK AGAIN
and Bella has a brush with a burglar
at 7.0

Radio Times, October 1954

"SOMEONE OUGHT TO SAY SOMETHING, DON'T YOU THINK?"

Men Only, July 1945

"*Yes, dear, I joined up to escape housework.*"

London Opinion,
December 1942

erroneous impression of the man. His name was Wade. He was small and grey-haired and could have easily been taken for a cashier in a large drapery store – or even a small one, for that matter. No fireball he, just a very gentle, relaxed little man in a grey three-piece, with socks and personality to match. His editorial den was compact to the point of claustrophobia. He was a super encouragement to me in those early days.

Tower House housed the offices of many magazines, all the products of publishers George Newnes and C. Arthur Pearson. *London Opinion, Men Only, Strand Magazine, Tit Bits, Wideworld, Country Life,* and *Westminster Gazette* were just some of the many popular titles produced by them. I met Reginald Arkell several times on my visits to Tower House. Arkell was, at that time, editor of *Men Only,* and occupied a small office adjoining *London Opinion.* He was also a popular playwright then, and had co-written the successful comedy *1066 and All That.* At the start of a freelance career you can easily be impressed by the halls of fame, or publishers' offices, but it must be said that Tower House had to me all the atmosphere of a warehouse. It was a paper treadmill from which poured a constant flood of reading matter and, thank heavens, commissions and much encouragement for this particular artist.

I once said to Wade how much I admired the work of Ronald Searle, and that I would like to meet him one day. I had no sooner expressed the desire than it was arranged. From the dust and cobwebs of my mind a faint notion tells me that I made my way around the Kensington area to find the then young bachelor's flat. A handsome, delicately featured man, he appeared surprisingly shy and modest to be the possessor of such a wealth of talent. When I arrived his drawing board was surrounded by discarded paper rolled into balls. He explained that he was trying to capture the face of some person who, it would seem, had little individuality. Eastern hieroglyphics above his light switch spelled out a message which, I believe, warned you in no uncertain terms about conserving energy. His studio flat was in one of those great Georgian houses which lent dignity to that area of London. The bathroom had a large Victorian bath with claw feet, and above the end of the bath a copper geyser of Heath Robinson design hung perilously on the wall. Peeping from behind the geyser, and over the edge of and around the bath, were girls of St Trinian's, all with evil leers and wide eyes peering into the bath – an excellent ploy by the artist to ensure no one held the bathroom beyond a reasonable time.

Searle at that time was only at the beginning of his brilliant career, and not long back from being an inmate of one of the most notorious and hellish of Japanese prison camps. The St Trinian's girls owe much to the prison camp's guards, and many cartoonists have gained inspiration from Searle's vigorously wicked line. I can see a strong affinity in the styles of Gerald Scarfe and Ralph Steadman. It was a great privilege to meet Searle then, and the next time I was to see him was when he appeared as an extra in a St Trinian's film. If you did not know him to see, you would easily have missed him, for he looked as though he had been forced on set. Definitely not a Hitchcock.

Another hero of mine, Leslie Illingworth, a superb cartoonist, proved to be a totally contrasting figure to Searle. Billy Glenn, who left the *Belfast Telegraph* to go to the London *Daily Mail*, was to be my contact with Illingworth. Billy was doing his Ballyscullion drawings for *Dublin Opinion* and was at that time strip editor for the *Mail*. One day I decided to call at the *Mail* and have a chat with him, and during our conversation, which flowed as only the talk of two Irishmen can when they have not met for a long time, Illingworth's name cropped up.

'You like his work?' asked Billy.

'I think he's a magnificent artist,' I replied.

'Would you like to meet him?' was the next question.

'Delighted,' said I.

I was taken forthwith to the lion's den. Lion he was – a burly character with great bushy eyebrows, and not unlike the film actor Thomas Mitchell, who had played Scarlett O'Hara's father in *Gone with the Wind*. I was introduced as a fellow artist.

'Rowel thinks you're a magnificent artist, Leslie,' said Billy.

The great man thrust out a huge hand and shook mine until my eyes were rolling in my head like a pinball machine. 'How right he is, how right he is,' boomed Illingworth.

Later, talking to Glenn, I laughingly referred to Illingworth's reactions. 'He was joking, of course,' I said.

'Joking my foot!' said Billy. 'He meant every word he said. Full of self-confidence!'

It takes all sorts – as the cliché goes.

From 1943 onwards, *Dublin Opinion* was my gateway to a new and exciting world, a world which differed so completely from the one that had spawned me in the North. In culture and in attitude the worlds

TÓSTAL NUMBER

DUBLIN April, 1954
Price Sixpence

The National
Humorous
Journal of
Ireland
OPINION

" And now I take this opportunity of welcoming those of our foreign visitors who happen to be in attendance at this, our special Tóstalelection."

"Ah, shure it'll do."

were well apart. The gracious Georgian buildings gave Dublin its dignity, with the Liffey and its Halfpenny Bridge, O'Connell Street, the GPO and the pillar with Nelson checking that his wallet was still in his inside pocket. Someone who did not like his lording it over the citizens later brought him down to earth. The mouths of the two rivers, the Liffey and the Lagan, in themselves voiced the differing characteristics of the two cities. All hustle, and bustle, clatter and clash, dramatically backlit by intermittent blue-white flashes from welders' flames at Harland and Wolff, the Lagan extended a boisterous welcome to Belfast. Whereas the Liffey, with its elegant eighteenth-century Custom House, the figure of hope on its green dome, sitting close to the river's edge, its reflection gently rippling on the quiet waters, a few boats from lands afar resting placidly on the quayside of that city of culture where the ghosts of past greatness are ever-present, has a voice much more seductive.

Dublin became a second home to me through my association with *Dublin Opinion*. It was an excellent magazine that grew from, and with, the South's independence. Born in March 1892, the brainchild of its first editor, Arthur Booth, with Thomas J. Collins and Charles E. Kelly, it operated successfully until its demise in 1972. Booth died in 1926, still a young man, and it was left to Tom Collins and Charlie Kelly to carry on, which they did with great effect until they too retired. It was very much their baby and even though artists like Bill Beckett (Maskee), Neil O'Kennedy (NO'K), Glenn, William Conn and myself contributed the bulk of its pictorial matter, none of us ever attained any degree of responsibility. Their love of the child was so great that its death was guaranteed upon their retirement. This was a great loss to Ireland. The magazine's slogan was 'humour is the safety valve of a nation', and now the valve was turned off. In 1977, 1978 and 1979 *Dublin Opinion* Christmas annuals were published in an attempt to resurrect the magazine. Unfortunately, no resurrection took place. Apart from their covers and titles, the pretenders bore little or no similarity to the original, and died of anaemia.

Up until 1943 I had been drawing mainly for English periodicals when the painter Theo Gracey mentioned my name to Charlie Kelly. This resulted in a welcome being extended to me, and I started to contribute on a regular basis to *Dublin Opinion*. I will never forget the thrill of my first visit to Middle Abbey Street and the offices. Just past an antique shop I found a doorway tucked into a little dark hallway. A sign informed me that my destination was the first floor. I made my way up the stairway to a small landing, turned left with the stairs and mounted a few more steps, and there it was, shining gold on the glass of a door – *Dublin Opinion*. The very distinctive letters fairly leaped at me. I cannot explain why, but I got more kick out of my first sight of that door than I did from visiting *Punch*. It could have been national pride – the prospect of being a part of Ireland's own *Punch* – or the feeling a rugby player must get when he runs onto the field, wearing his green jersey for the first time.

The office was spacious and bright, and had a large bay window with, again, the magazine's name proudly emblazoned upon it. Outside the window and across the street the offices of the *Irish Independent* stood in full view. A strong smell of cigarette smoke pervaded the air. The source of it sat Buddha-like behind a very large and heavy desk that was littered with papers. Tom Collins was short and plump and was a chain-smoker. Empty Sweet Afton packets were strewn around in abundance, his ashtrays were overflowing with cigarette stubs, and his dark three-piece suit was pepper-dotted with ash. He had a round, pale face with full red lips, and dark eyes that protruded from very moist underlids.

Occasionally a plump nicotined finger would wipe a tear from his cheek. His hair, dark and lank, angled in a forelock part-way down his brow. The dark eyes would remain fixed on you without, so it seemed, a blink; the constancy of his stare would be broken for an instant, now and then, when he would slowly raise his eyes ceilingwards. No doubt a thought was running through his head, an idea, perhaps, for another humorous article. He always reminded me of Vichy France's Pierre Laval, *sans* moustache and *sans* deviousness. This was Tom, a very serious gentleman with an outward appearance that effectively concealed the humour within.

From Laurel and Hardy to Mutt and Jeff, you would never have found two more contrasting types than Tom Collins and Charlie Kelly: Tom, short, plump and dark, and Charlie shooting off in a skywards direction. Well in excess of six feet, with a long thin face on a very long neck and a most pronounced Adam's apple, he exuded friendship. He always had a great wide smile and a great hand extended – possible requisites for his position as director of Radio Éireann. Bespectacled, light of hair, both in volume and in colour, the long fellow fairly bubbled with enthusiasm for the job in hand. Tom, every bit as keen and enthusiastic, and indeed as friendly, held his emotions in check.

Charlie had two brothers in the priesthood, Phelim and Honorious. Honorious became a good friend of mine when he was appointed to Ardoyne parish in Belfast. He, like Charlie, was tall and also like Tom in that he smoked like a factory chimney. Unlike Tom, however, he was aware of cigarette ash and how it affected dark clothing, and he had a spontaneous habit of dusting himself down from head to toe after every few drags of the weed. Honorious and myself were useful messengers between the capitals for Charlie. On the many occasions when I had to visit the office in Middle Abbey Street, my weekends were spent in the Wicklow Hotel or Jury's. Later I had the pleasure of being adopted by Charlie and his lovely wife Kathleen. At Avoca Avenue, Blackrock, I spent many happy weekends with the Kelly family, despite the convent bells across the way, which could, at times, disturb your early morning slumber. Due to *Dublin Opinion*, I got to know many people and thousands got to know me.

By my *Dublin Opinion* association, I gained an open sesame to the press world. In the mid-1950s I was invited to do a series of illustrations for the *Irish Times* by that great editor Douglas Gageby, whose friendship

I will always value. Douglas had the knack of making you feel good and also the gift of creating a relaxed atmosphere. Time seemed to be under his control. He had the foresight, if he scented any vestige of ability, to grab it for the paper, adding to his strong team of specialists. Some twenty years after that initial spell of illustrating, and following the demise of *Dublin Opinion*, Douglas and I met in the Wellington Park Hotel in Belfast. This chance meeting rekindled past memories and Douglas asked me if I would be interested in drawing for the *Irish Times* again. I did not have to be talked into it, and from that time forward a long and pleasant association developed. Douglas, now retired, will be enjoying his fishing and, I have no doubt, will be making a lot of good catches, as he did in the newspaper world.

I also had a long period in the late 1950s with the *Irish Press*, edited by Conor O'Brien. Unfortunately this happened following the death of my very good friend Bill Beckett, who had been doing a regular series for the *Press*. Stepping into Bill's shoes was not the easiest thing to do and it was certainly one of the saddest. Conor O'Brien and I got on extremely well, and again I had a long run with a top Irish paper. Conor moved from the *Press* to the *Sunday Independent*, in whose employment he was to die, a relatively young man. A cricket enthusiast, he used to ask me to do covers for match programmes when they had special international-style confrontations in Dublin. Before Conor joined the *Sunday Independent*, Hector Legge, the editor, had me drawing a series for that paper. I moved around a lot before joining the *Belfast Telegraph*.

My first work for the *Belfast Telegraph* was published in December 1936 when I was the winner of its Christmas drawing competition – 'grade 5, boys and girls, 13–17 years'. When I was called into their offices in Royal Avenue as their very nervous first prizewinner, I never could have foreseen the long and successful association I was to have with the paper. In the early 1950s I started to do single-column topical cartoons, titled 'Newslant', which appeared as many times a week as the news inspired. From these grew the larger feature cartoon which, after a few minor editorial skirmishes, gave me complete freedom of expression. There is no thrill greater than seeing your work appear on the printed page and no greater stimulus than the reader's approbation. On this score, the *Telegraph* proved to be an excellent confidence-booster. I left my friends in the *Telegraph* in 1990 to join the oldest paper in Europe, the *Belfast News-Letter*, now called the *News Letter*.

"Well, what do you think Sarge, is it or is it not likely to cause a breach of the peace?"

Belfast Telegraph,
February 1954

14

RUNNING THE GAUNTLET

MY LATE FRIEND THEO GRACEY, who made regular trips to Dublin, seemed to have as many connections as the local telephone exchange. A keen amateur wartime smuggler, he endeared himself to many by his 'tea and sugar' runs. Plump of girth, he never minded adding two or three pounds on a trip. Under his shirt he wore a cloth belt, which was divided into pockets, each containing alternately packets of tea and sugar. During the war years, rationing had up-valued these commodities in the South to the status of gold dust. Return runs were on the 'sausage express', when Theo and thousands more would be laden with Hafner's best.

Photographic printing paper was scarce in the North but Theo kept supplies healthy. One occasion springs to mind when things did not go quite smoothly for the contraband conspirator. He had bought up a bargain load of Kodak printing paper from some source in Dublin, and using his persuasive powers, of which he had more than a fair share, he enlisted the aid of his three travelling companions. I was one of those soldiers. Each of us devised our own methods of hoodwinking the customs. Being a raw beginner, I simply packed the three vibrant yellow boxes in between the shirts in my suitcase. My nerves went to hell as soon as I had those boxes in hand; their colour seemed luminous to me and I imagined, should my case be opened, the area would be bathed in sunlight, and another case would be opened several weeks later with myself on a smuggling charge. Lord preserve me from the conscience of a transgressor – a cowardly one, at that. Once on the train, Gracey settled down with a smiling face, the epitome of innocence. Perhaps a better student of character would have adjudged it a trifle too beatific to be believable. The other two, who shall be nameless because I cannot recall who they were, got their heads behind the evening papers. Whether it is just to embellish the story, or whether my memory for detail serves me well – anyhow, one of the newspapers trembled, and the compartment was airless.

The train pulled out of Amiens Street (now Connolly) station, and began to make its way north. Theo, a contented man, completely relaxed, gazed out at the passing scene, with the two newspapers still covering our fellow conspirators. I sat staring at all three, mentally trying to total up our potential sentences. I leaned across and informed Theo that my instincts told me that something would go wrong. Within myself I felt my greatest need was a confessional, despite my Protestant upbringing. My mentor – or more correctly under the circumstances, my tormentor – assured me all would be plain sailing.

Too soon we were at Dundalk. A detachment of uniformed officers started boarding our train, and into our carriage came an officious little man, whose peaked cap seemed to be held in position by the bridge of a rather long blueish nose and two shocking-pink ears. To my mind he looked mean, even vicious, and he had all the appearance of being foul-tempered. I could have hated him if I had not been so scared. Obviously my eyes telegraphed a guilt-ridden conscience, because the little fiend made straight for me. I froze, as men of conscience have been known to do when guilty.

'Anything to declare? Open up!' he snapped. The double statement at once indicated to me that he could read eyes. 'Open up', sounded like 'come clean'.

From behind the back of my interrogator, Theo tick-tacked the information that I should open my case. The yellow boxes made the searcher's face light up.

'What are these?' he barked.

'They're, um, ah, boxes of paper I have to draw on' was the utterly ludicrous reply.

No fool was this officer. 'Let's have a look.'

I detected a certain dry quality in the voice. He proceeded, with what I suspected to be sadistic satisfaction, to unwrap the printing paper, thus exposing it to the light. Theo's face remained expressionless, while two worried countenances hung above the news headlines.

'Right,' said Bluenose, 'here you are.'

He tossed the useless packets of paper back to me. The two news

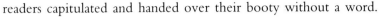

readers capitulated and handed over their booty without a word.

Master Smuggler Gracey remained unperturbed and when questioned calmly said, 'Nothing to declare.'

Upon a thorough search he was found to be clean. No doubt this was a surprise to the brass-buttoned sniffer dog, but it was an even greater surprise to the three stooges. We knew he, personally, had at least eight boxes when we boarded that train. With a shrug of the shoulders and a very hard look at me, the conscientious customs man marched off with half a dozen sealed boxes of Kodak bromide. Once we thought he was out of sight, I whispered an apology to the Smuggler King.

'Don't worry, all is not lost,' he smiled.

'How come?' I asked, leaning across the better to hear his reply.

'I managed to store them away in a cabinet in the gents,' he said, with a smug grin. 'They are quite safe. No one will find them there.'

This he said as I happened to glance out of the window. 'Want to bet?' I queried.

He looked askance. 'What are you getting at?' he said, for the first time indicating the slightest discomfort.

I nodded out of the window. There he was, cap on blue nose and pink ears, marching triumphantly along the platform with arms lovingly clutching eight yellow boxes.

A few years following that fiasco I had a brush with the selfsame son of Satan. I was down at an ideas conference in *Dublin Opinion*, and I thought I would bring back a half-bottle of brandy to my elder brother, Bill. Confidence had grown a bit through close study of Theo and his carefree approach to this minor felony. I stuck the half-bottle in my case and boarded the express without the slightest of qualms. When the train started from Amiens Street, so did the customs search. We were just beyond Drogheda when IT appeared, nose nearer purple and ears still assisting in holding the cap. Whether he recognised me or not, I will never know, but he made no bones about wanting to examine my case. I opened it at once and told him I had a half-bottle of brandy for my brother.

'You can't take it across,' he snapped.

'It's only a half-bottle. I thought you were allowed a certain amount,' I countered.

'You'll have to pay duty. Come off with me at Dundalk and fill in a form.'

'I don't wish to do that,' I said. 'If I can't take it over, I'll take it here.'

He looked stunned. I slowly unscrewed the metal top, put the bottle to my lips and started to lower the molten liquid. A few gasps for breath, both from myself and a pop-eyed bluenose, and I rapidly lowered the half-bottle. Hardly the way to treat brandy, or one's self, but it was almost worth it to see the frustration and disbelief on boyo's face, a face that, without doubt, would have enjoyed the swigs more than I did. He marched off much as he had done on that previous occasion when he found Gracey clean. In those days I did not drink at all, so it is quite understandable that, when the train arrived in Belfast, I certainly did not march off. How I got off, I know not, and how I got home could only have been by a miracle.

On one of my frequent visits to Dublin, when the train fare was two pounds ten shillings return, I arrived early for an appointment and had about an hour in hand. The fact that rain was bouncing from the pavements, like silver knitting needles creating their little patterns of liquid circles, suggested I search for shelter to pass the time. My rapid footsteps took me to an art gallery. The exhibition was away beyond me and, I had no doubt, many others. Many others would not perhaps admit to such ignorance, but I have a touch of the George Washington malady and, thus afflicted, cannot think of a quick excuse. The works on show were very abstract and the illustrated catalogue cost two pounds which, at the time, also seemed a trifle avant-garde. Needless to say, I did not purchase a catalogue but simply mooched round the gallery. There were striped canvasses, spotted ones, plain blue, white, green, and some whereon paint had been spilled. All were somewhat huge, both in area and in price. As I circumnavigated the rooms, I saw a man standing before a huge canvas upon which, in dead centre, was an area of very mixed colours, as though the artist had tripped and dropped his palette on it. The man who was viewing this contemporary catastrophe held his catalogue tightly pressed to his bosom. To say he was bemused would not be incorrect. As I looked over his shoulder at the contribution to his mental confusion, I blasphemously, though involuntarily, gasped, 'Jesus Christ!'

The man swung round, his eyes wide in wonder and admiration. 'How did you know?' he asked.

On another occasion, this time in London, I was with friends who wished to see the famous bricks they, as taxpayers, had purchased. We went to the Tate Gallery and, on entering, we saw some rusty scaffolding with a green tarpaulin draped eccentrically over it. My friends, assuming I was a most knowledgeable character in all art forms, asked me what the work represented.

'How do I know?' I asked defensively. 'If I knew the title, perhaps I could work out some explanation. I'll ask the attendant.' I went straight to one of those terribly important-looking men in warder's uniform. Pointing to the problem, I said, 'What does that mean?'

'That, sir, means they're fixing a bloody leak in the roof' was the enlightening answer.

15

THE ACADEMY AND WILLIAM CONOR

WHILE STUDYING PART-TIME AT THE college of art in the late 1930s, I had been invited to join the Ulster Academy of Arts. The academy had beautiful rooms in the Old Museum at College Square North, a building that had all the dignity of the Georgian period. A spiral staircase set between two large Georgian windows led up to the music gallery, where a glass dome in the roof supplied extra light. I was thrilled to be part of what was recognised as the only organised artists' body in Northern Ireland. It was started by a group of enthusiasts in the 1800s, when it was called the Ulster Ramblers' Club. In 1930 it became the Ulster Academy of Arts, and twenty years later was granted the royal prefix, to become the Royal Ulster Academy.

Before the Ulster Academy of Arts had its royal prefix to adorn the title, it was a much less professional body than it now is. More socially active, it met regularly twice a week for studio evenings, when painting sessions and other forms of entertainment were enjoyed. Two exhibitions a year were presented: a spring show, when there was no selection and it was not obligatory to frame works; and the much more prestigious autumn show, where frames added lustre to the scene. Standards fluctuated as selection was casual, and criticism flourished. Impervious to the broadsides, the old barque ploughed on through those stormy seas of ridicule to become what it is today.

The studio evenings were the responsibility of whichever member cared to volunteer for the title of convener of the sub-committee. This important post could be held for several years if the incumbent showed no signs of weakening or if (and this was highly likely) no volunteers were forthcoming. I can recall a council meeting once when the chair

116

Old Museum, College Square North, where the Ulster Academy of Arts had its rooms (Courtesy of National Library of Ireland)

was occupied by Tom Drummond, honorary treasurer, a damask designer by profession and a Scot by birth. He had a jolly and bouncing personality that was offset by the countenance of the honorary secretary on his right, James Ferry. Ferry had a long florid face stamped with an expression of perpetual disdain. When we sought an answer to any problems relating to our premises at the Old Museum, his answer was always in the negative: 'We've tried it all before, sir. The architects won't budge.' That was his stock answer, which naturally enough convinced us that the architects were a stubborn lot of whatshisnames.

The rest of the council consisted of Maurice Wilks, sucking on his pipe, R.C. Blair, who with the honorary treasurer and the honorary secretary made up a trio of damask designers, the immaculate Max McCabe, Ian and myself. One evening we had just got through the apologies and were starting into the agenda proper when a stranger entered, apologised for being late, and took a seat at the table. I had not seen him before and enquired of Ian if the stranger was a co-opted

117

member. Ian knew him not and asked Wilks, who quizzed Max, who in turn got no satisfaction from R.C. The meeting plodded on, as many of those meetings could do, with trivialities being discussed *ad nauseam*. The stranger was the most interested member of council. Our last item on the agenda, and in the chairman's opinion the most important, was the election for convener of the sub-committee.

'Any volunteers?' he asked, his eyes scanning the faces, faces that had eyes averted in every direction barring that of the chair. The chair, however, caught a pair of optics that he imagined reflected a search for knowledge. 'You, sir,' said the chairman hopefully, 'would you take it on?'

'What does it entail?' enquired the source of hope.

'Well, you just organise studio evenings, painting sessions, and arrange for a nude model,' said the chair, making it sound as simple as he could.

A look of utter perplexity registered on Hope's face. 'Excuse me, but is this not the Belfast Naturalists' Field Club?'

He was a stranger and we nearly took him in. That was how casual the academy could be in those early days.

The academy then was comprised of an academic body of twenty academicians, twenty associates, and a hundred-odd ordinary members – some extremely odd, and many very ordinary. Of the lot, only a few could claim professional status. The academy received a lot of criticism, some fair, some unfair, just as it does to this day. But then, were not academies made for critics? I was not long in that august body before I was elected an associate and a member of council. This was another accolade, being part of the board of management as it were, although it bore more relationship to a ladies' knitting circle. Being a callow youth, I was neither confident enough nor audacious enough to tell my world-weary fellow councillors that they drivelled overmuch.

My friends then were wise men who were not on the council and seldom appeared at the academy: William Conor, Frank McKelvey, Theo Gracey and Echlin Neill – from all of them I learned a lot. From Conor, humility and truth. From McKelvey, self-values and professionalism. Theo Gracey passed on the gift of enjoying everything around, and finding fun in all things. They are all dead now, the last to go being Echlin Neill, who remained my staunchest supporter and mentor until his death in 1981 at the age of ninety-three.

When I was eventually elected a full academician in 1953, some changes had taken place, and a lot of younger blood had been injected.

Taylor and Ruby Carson's wedding day, 19 February 1949; *left to right:* Rowland Hill, Theo Gracey, Taylor and Ruby, John Galway and Maurice Wilks

The transfusion included many forward-looking types, revolutionaries, in those days – people like Max and Gladys McCabe, Desmond Turner, Maurice Wilks, John Turner, J.C. Blair, Taylor Carson and Ian, all anxious to make changes. They elected William Conor as president, and myself as vice-president, an office that no longer exists. The reason for the creation of a vice-president was to ensure that there would always be someone to preside, as Conor was not at all a keen attender. The presidential chair and the chain of office were a bore to him. To put it in his own words, he 'felt a right oul' cod sittin' up there with thon contraption roun' my neck'.

William Conor was one of the most sincere men I have ever known, who had a sensitivity and a memory for the past that few could equal. His was a friendship I will always treasure. He was a man who, though gentle and modest, could criticise with a biting wit. Never malicious,

119

if Billy disliked anyone he simply gave them a wide berth. Excess William Conor
modesty was possibly his greatest fault, and he placed little value on his
own work, preferring to give his paintings away rather than discuss
prices. With whatever little money he had, he was careful, though he
could be most generous with his paintings.

Billy had an exhibition in CEMA's Donegall Place gallery in 1950 and,
as always, his collected works gave me and many others great pleasure.
At that time I was in Fisherwick Dramatic Society and there I spread the
word of how good the show was, advising the members not to miss
seeing it. My friend Yvonne Henderson, who had not as yet considered
me a contender for her hand, expressed a great deal more interest than

our other fellow players. When she went to the exhibition, she was greatly impressed. Remarkably, although Yvonne and I did discuss the show, we never expressed any hint of personal preferences. Sitting with Billy in Campbell's coffee bar in Donegall Square North several days after the close of his exhibition, I was asked if I had a favourite among his pieces there. I told him I would find it difficult to be emphatic but that I was struck by a small oil entitled *The Waiting Room*. I thought it exceptionally well painted. This appeared to please him greatly because, he said, that was one of his own favourites. It was a few months after our conversation in Campbell's that Yvonne met Billy for the first time. During their conversation, he asked her which painting she had liked best in his exhibition, and she reacted much like myself. She too had liked many but, amazingly, had fallen for *The Waiting Room*.

Months passed and turned into a couple of years. Yvonne's charms had by then captivated me and succeeded in getting me onto my knees, and we had completed plans for the big day. The wedding presents formed a pyramid in the bride-to-be's sitting-room and, standing out from the great assortment of kind thoughts was *The Waiting Room*. Two people had on separate occasions expressed their preference for a particular painting, and after a passage of two years, Billy remembered.

The old hands in Allen's confided in me that Conor was a big hit with the ladies in his young days. Even though he always remained a bachelor, I could well imagine him to have been quite a lad in his youth. When I first met him he was to my teenage mind an 'oul' fella'. He encouraged this misconception by referring to himself constantly as 'only an oul' cod'. What a character he was and what a figure he cut. His was an unmistakable image in the street when he hove in sight, with his black wide-brimmed hat, its brim elementally corrugated through countless years of wear, his blue shirt, with collar slightly frayed, and a heavy knitted black silk bow tie that appeared permanently weighted to the right. As he walked, Billy always seemed to incline his head slightly to the right, and whether it was this propensity that influenced the bow, or the bow's weight that dictated the inclination of his head, one can only guess. His overcoat was raglan, black and roomy, reaching as near his ankles as made no matter, and from the wide sleeves only the tips of his fingers showed. His gait was slow and his general appearance was of someone who was pondering a problem. That he was pondering was quite likely, because his mind outpaced his step. Conor missed little on his peregrinations; he observed and retained every little idiosyncrasy of those who peopled his world. From these observations Ireland became the richer. Billy had no time for hypocrisy, pomposity, fools, critics or abstract art. Once, he told me that he never imagined there was such intellectual depth and meaning to his pictures until he read some critic who pronounced it so. 'Damn it, Rowel, it's wonderful what we're capable of and don't realise it,' he quipped. Though never one to ridicule another, he was a very shrewd judge of character. He despised vulgarity and know-alls, and would say, 'You know, I never realised how much I depend on people who can't paint to explain my work to me.'

When Conor was in Allen's, they drew, not on plates, but special stones. He was known as a black man. This was nothing to do with the Orange Order, but was the person entrusted with the black in the poster. Being the drawing colour, this was most important, and it required great expertise in order to create a wide range of tone values. When the other colours were printed, the black would be added last and the quality of the finished product depended mainly on it.

I once asked Billy did he know how he got his style.

'Damn it, Rowel, I never gave it a thought,' said he.

I then launched into my theory of how that unique watercolour crayon technique was born. When he went sketching, Billy would always have some litho crayons in his pocket, being a black man. Old habits die hard, so he would sketch out his composition with the crayon. Having thus drawn his picture, he then added watercolour, which would be repelled by the grease of the crayon, thereby producing that uniquely personal style of his. Many fakes exist today that are instantly recognisable in that many are drawn with wax crayons, giving an entirely different texture to the work. Litho crayons were available in many grades, like pencils, from hard to very soft. They could be used like pencils, and were much more subtle than the coarse, unsympathetic wax. Wax crayons are lumpy on surfaces, whilst the lithographic crayon is bland and works smoothly into the grain.

To think that I used to sell crayon and watercolour drawings by Conor for fifteen guineas each makes me shudder now. When any friend expressed the desire to have a Conor, I would oblige by going straight to Billy. He would quote twelve or fifteen, but I always stuck to fifteen guineas, and he would say, 'Damn it, Rowel, you're very decent. I must

122

stand you a cup of coffee sometime.' His life was frugal. He and his brother Russell lived in a large, gloomy and shabby terrace house in Salisbury Avenue, off the Antrim Road. On a cold evening the brothers would, fully overcoated, sit hunched over a double-barred electric fire that had only one bar functioning and that sparked furiously and ominously from time to time. Often when I visited them I found they had nothing to eat. On such occasions I would go out, buy some provisions and prepare a meal for them. At times like this you had to watch Russell carefully as he now lived in a cerebral wonderland. Danger lurked when removing dishes from him. You had to wait until he had turned away from his plate, which always shone like a diamond, he having polished it with his last slice of bread. Any attempt to remove that plate before he had demolished the meal to his own satisfaction could well result in your hand being impaled by a fork. Feeding him required a lot of patience and an equal amount of vigilance. His senility was unpredictable; one moment he could be courteous and gentlemanly, the next, short-tempered and dependable as a bomb with a faulty fuse.

A select group used to gather for coffee and talk in Campbell's coffee bar, and later in the Chalet d'Or in Fountain Lane. I christened them the shadow cabinet. The regulars were Conor, John Hewitt, Jim Ryan, Jimmy Vitty, Sam Hanna Bell, Denis Ireland and Joe Tomelty. The literati, men of the theatre, and painters were drawn as filings to a magnet. It was a meeting place worthy of Dr Johnson, and akin to the Pearl Bar in Dublin where similar worthies would hold court. On this particular day of which I speak, there were but few of us in session, Billy included. Upon the scene there entered a particular artist for whom Billy had little love. The said artist was cynical, hare-brained, not the most congenial of company, nor had he the best of manners. Without waiting for a break in the conversation, he launched into an attack on the government, the arts council, and any other target he could bring to a rebellious mind. Then, just as suddenly as he had started, he applied the brakes with a half-apology.

'Ach, I suppose I'm my own worst enemy,' he announced to a stunned group.

Conor, the first to recover, leaned forward and said, 'Oh now, wait a minute, wait a minute – not while I'm alive.'

This, I was later informed, is not an original retort, but it was the first time I had heard it, and it was so typical of Conor that I cannot imagine that he was deliberately quoting someone else.

Conor's studio, situated opposite the Belfast Museum and Art Gallery on the Stranmillis Road, was the authentic artist's den. It had plenty of space and a glass roof, and was furnished with a large heavy easel (which he eventually bequeathed to me). Canvases and boards were scattered in heaps around the walls with reckless abandon, and there was a small table he used as a palette. A strange assortment of tins, buckets, saucers and dishes, eccentrically arranged, occupied much of the floor space. On a wet day they came into their own when they supplied atmospheric background music as raindrops from a leaking roof fell, each to its own ordained receptacle. On a very wet day, you could be lulled into a dream-like state with the plink, plonk, pling of that water music. Billy would be working away happily to the sound of this incidental music until – splat, splat, splat – when he would spring into action shouting, 'My God, a leak!' as though this were something really new. 'I must find something to stop it,' he would say, and start ferreting around until he eventually unearthed a suitable container. This would quite naturally change the whole orchestral arrangement. Billy would rub his hands with satisfaction for a job well done then, adjusting the long blue smock that kept sliding off his shoulder like a troublesome ball gown, he would return to chronicle the life and times of his people.

Conor's deep and sincere love of Ireland and its people burned from his work like the flame of the unknown warrior – unquenchable, everlasting. To my mind, this strong love for his native land made him

124

our greatest artist. His studies of the people, their work and play, the transport they used, from jaunting cars to tram cars, recorded indelibly his period of the twentieth century. These impressions (for impressionist he was) made him a pictorial historian. Those loving observations of mill-workers and shipbuilders, bare-footed, clogged or guttied, place him on a special pedestal amongst our historical recorders.

He used to tell one story concerning an occasion when he was sitting sketching at the River Lagan. 'It was a nice day and the scene attracted me. The trees' dark reflections added to the beauty of glinting sunlight on the water's surface. As I settled down to enjoy the scene, a small dog appeared. It made a damn nuisance of itself rubbing up against me, tail-wagging and barking. I kept trying to chase it away. It's a most difficult thing to paint with a dog constantly butting your arm and demanding attention.' Apparently, after some barking on his own behalf, Billy eventually saw the dog off. He continued undisturbed for an hour or so and finally completed the watercolour to his own satisfaction. He placed the finished work against a nearby tree and stood back to admire it. Suddenly, from out of the surrounding shrubbery, the pestilent pup reappeared. It looked at the watercolour, sniffed it and, raising a back leg, added a finishing wash. Billy summed up this story by saying, 'It must have been a damn critic!' What a lot it tells us of the man's nature when he could laugh in the face of disaster.

16

PEN PORTRAITS

FRANK McKELVEY STOOD BACK to view his canvas. Elegantly poised with the palette tilted on his left forearm and his brush held aloft, he gave the dignified impression of the conductor of a symphony orchestra. The one incongruity to mar his image was the cigarette dangling from his lips. Three-quarters of the weed consisted of grey ash which curved gently floorwards, while blue smoke spiralled slowly upwards. One wondered how much of a cigarette McKelvey smoked when he was painting and how much the cigarette actually smoked itself. A couple of buttons on his beige cardigan undone. his bow tied to perfection, and his shirt immaculate, he looked much more the prosperous businessman than the popular conception of an artist. This impression was hardly surprising, because he was one of a rare species – an artist who was a shrewd businessman. Frank knew his market and his capabilities as an artist, both of which were considerable. A superb painter of the Irish landscape, and a portrait painter in constant demand, he was at his happiest with the easel before him.

It was when I was at the college of art that I first met Frank McKelvey. I had heard of him when I was an apprentice in S.C. Allen's. In the artists' room they used to talk with great reverence about the greats who used to work at lithography. Names, names, names: Sir Frank Brangwyn, Sir D.Y. Cameron, Sir Russell Flint, and on and on *ad infinitum*. However, when they got down to locals, the Allen's lithographers spoke of them in terms which, to the young apprentice, verged on idolatry. We heard of Matt Sanford, the caricaturist; the Morrows, famous for their theatrical posters; and many others of whom I have never heard, before or since. Of those artists who had attained varying degrees of notoriety, none quite achieved the virtual canonisation of

126

William Conor and Frank McKelvey.

My introduction to Frank, as I recall, was through the irrepressible and kindly Theo Gracey. It was during a period when I was helping Theo out with his workload of commercial art. He had a studio, in Queen Street, in partnership with another commercial artist, Andy Long. First impressions of that studio would have panicked the calmest of natures. There were papers everywhere in mad confusion, reference books and magazines scattered about at random – a room of horrifying disarray which, oddly enough, seemed to cause no confusion whatsoever to the partners, who could find anything they wanted simply by reaching out a hand in a predestined direction. A strong odour of film developer chemicals hung in the air, coming from the tiny darkroom the partners used to make their photographic plates.

Theo did a lot of outdoor sketching and it was when he was arranging an outing with Frank that he took me round to the master's studio in Howard Street. From the dark to the light, from a junk room to the studied tidiness of a doctor's consulting room, the contrast in character of the two men was made immediately obvious simply by walking from one studio to another. Even though I knew Frank to be an artist, when I was introduced I thought him more like a consultant physician. Dignity personified, a gentleman of elegant appearance and manners, McKelvey was as far removed from the Bohemian image as is the pope.

127

He was a private person. Some thought him aloof, but if you were accepted as a friend, the friendship was for life. I am flattered to have been considered a friend of his and taken into his family circle.

After meeting Frank with Theo and going with him on their sketching trips, I started modelling for him. Greater love hath no man than that he can endure modelling for his friend. Frank got so many portraits to paint – of doctors, professors and so on – and many of those notables had so little time to sit that it was necessary to have someone model the gowns. Bravely I volunteered, and for art's sake many the ache I suffered, from creaking necks to bodily cramps. The whole effort was very worth while because Frank talked a lot and thus you learned a lot. In this way I was rewarded for my pains.

He was most amusing when discussing a finished painting. 'I rather like this area here,' he would say, pointing to one section of the picture. 'I stroked the soft brush over it and got that quite nice misty little touch. Don't you think the reflected light is most effective on this figure, and look here, don't the cows in this field make an interesting composition, with two standing and one sitting?' Frank would calmly eulogise upon section after section as though it were the work of another. No area was overlooked in his analysis – a sort of praising by numbers. When he had finished his observations and you had put all his summations together, it was then you realised that you must be looking at something extra special. It was funny to think that Frank's enthusiasm for the work in hand and his complete absorption in it rendered him unconscious of the fact that he was actually acclaiming his own genius. Frank could never be accused of boasting, but he was always a great man for pointing out 'rather nice little touches' in his own work, as indeed he could with the works of others.

I remember him asking me once when he saw me working in the garden, if I had insured my hands. I told him no, and was instantly given a dressing-down for doing such heavy work as digging at the peril of damaging my hands. To this day I do not know whether or not he had his own hands insured. However, I do remember, about a month or so after his lecture to me, seeing him hammering and banging and laying crazy paving in his garden, with his own bare hands.

A funny thing happened on the way to the Hibernian! Frank and I were going down via the *Enterprise* to the opening of the Royal Hibernian Academy. When the train got to Drogheda, Frank expressed a desire to freshen up, as he felt some grime was filtering in through the partially opened window. He retired to do his necessary retouching. After about ten minutes he reappeared looking somewhat bemused, shirt collar open and his bow tie dangling in his hand.

''s rather ridiculous, Rowel,' he said, smiling sheepishly, 'but I can't get my bow on.'

'What do you mean, you can't get it on?' I asked.

'I don't know,' he replied. 'I have tied it perfectly round the pipe in the toilet several times, but I can't manage it on myself.'

'Heavens, you've been tying bows since they were invented.'

'I know, but I seem suddenly to have lost the knack.'

I thought for a moment he had said 'neck' and was being funny. This was not the case, so he asked me if I could tie it for him. I was not sure, but tried it on the luggage rack and succeeded. However, when it came to trying the same thing on Frank, I failed hopelessly. As we neared Dublin, panic set in, and the task was given up as a bad job. Frank turned his coat collar up as we arrived in Amiens Street and we slunk off to the Wicklow Hotel with him looking like an undercover agent. At the hotel he went straight to his room and in about two minutes he came down smiling, bow perfectly tied. 'Damned funny, that,' says he.

After one of our sketching trips, I had painted an oil of a Killinchy farmstead. Frank liked it and said he would do a swap for one of his. We agreed an exchange. Frank got my picture, but a lapse of memory on both our parts saw me deprived of a McKelvey. When the Queen's University Festival started, the director Michael Emmerson invited me to have a one-man show in the foyer of the Whitla Hall at the university. As I never have many pictures lying around, this entailed borrowing. I asked Frank to lend me *Killinchy Farmstead*, which he willingly did. That was the last he saw of it because during the run of the festival, the picture was stolen from the show. Many years later my nephew told me of how he had been in Dublin with his daughter at a party in someone's flat, where he saw a landscape of mine. On questioning him, I suspected the picture to be the missing *Killinchy*. About five or six years after that incident I was approached by the Davis Gallery in Dublin to have a one-man show in its Capel Street premises. I resisted to the best of my ability, but succumbed to the blandishments of Gerald Davis. The show was duly arranged, and Gerald offered his flat to myself, my wife Yvonne and our son Jeremy. We arrived at his Bohemian sanctum and there, gracing Gerald's wall, was the missing picture.

'That's McKelvey's picture,' I said in amazement.

'No, it's not,' said Davis, 'it's yours.'

'It's McKelvey's,' I insisted.

It took a while before logic prevailed and Gerald realised I meant that the picture belonged to Frank McKelvey, though painted by myself. I told him it had been stolen. He was appalled, and said he had bought it years before in a Dublin auction. He hoped I would not take it from him. How could I? It was no longer my property, and with Frank having since died, it would have been tasteless to pursue the matter.

The wartime sketching trips with Theo Gracey were fun. Everywhere we went, Theo did a shopping expedition round local farms. Rationing, and trying to counteract same, was the name of his game. He stocked up with anything he could buy before he settled down to painting. When dusk started to descend we would pack up and start the drive home. Theo, full of bonhomie, would start singing at the top of his lungs, 'Nearer, my God, to Thee', or 'Steal away to Jesus'. He got so carried away with his vocal renderings, he would throw his head back and close his eyes. At times like this, and at the speed he drove, I was inclined to close my own eyes and pray that Jesus would not want us to steal away prematurely.

Sometimes, when I was helping Theo out, his studio door would burst open to admit the terror of the art world. He was small, wore a black flattish hat pulled down close to his eyes, hair stuck out all around like straw from a bin. A bow tie dangled sloppily under his chin. His mouth, drawn in a perpetual tight line, co-ordinated perfectly with the glint in his eyes. The dark overcoat he wore reached to about four inches from the ground and had all the appearance of a bell tent. His purpose for these sudden visitations was generally to give full vent to his contempt for the contemporary scene. The walking stick that he carried was neither a stylish embellishment nor an aid to walking, but was used most efficiently to clear a way through the crowds. Hurling abuse at anyone in his path, the little tyrant would slash his way through the human jungle like a South American native with a machete. His name, which struck terror into many a timid soul, was Langtry Lynas. I first came across his name in a book that he published himself and had printed in S.C. Allen's, called *The Hounds of Hell*. It contained

illustrations in black and white of humans in tortured confusion, which seemed strongly influenced by the works of Blake. Langtry's tongue was as lethal as his walking stick and few escaped a lashing.

I can recall once sitting in on an academy spring exhibition showing at the then CEMA gallery in Donegall Place. As per form, not a lot of art lovers were on the move that day. To my slight consternation, and only slight, because I got on reasonably well with him, the Tiny Terror materialised. Down the room I caught a glimpse of the writer John D. Stewart making himself scarce behind one of the screens.

I looked up to Langtry, because I was sitting, and said laughingly, 'Well, Mr Lynas, are you in to criticise?'

He pulled himself up a couple of centimetres, looked straight into my eyes and replied, 'I don't criticise – I condemn', turned on his heel and started his round of the show.

I noticed John D. doing some smart evasive work amongst the screens. Alas, like the fox, he was caught at last. One wrong step and his waistcoat buttons were face to face with Langtry Lynas. He looked down and gave a friendly greeting. Langtry's head went back and he glared at the ill-at-ease Mr Stewart. Instead of returning the greeting, which would have been uncharacteristic anyway, Langtry said in an uncomfortably loud voice, 'I'm surprised that a man of your intelligence should look at such a lot of shite.' Hardly the most subtle of criticism but certainly a devastating condemnation.

Obviously not a person to mince words, he was at the opening of a Conor exhibition in the same gallery. Bursting at the seams with notables – John Hewitt, Sam Hanna Bell, Zoltan Frankl, et al., – the show was being opened by Lynn Doyle, Conor's good friend. It was a very dignified occasion, with the quiet murmur of enlightened conversation filling the air, smiling faces, affable nods, and an atmosphere of sophistication and very civilised good behaviour.

Conor sat at a table with Lynn Doyle, trying hard to emulate the invisible man. The chairman banged on the table and suddenly it was the eleventh hour of the eleventh day of the eleventh month. Silence created, Lynn Doyle was introduced and with great dignity arose and proceeded to present his opening address. To a rapt audience he eulogised Billy Conor and his works, Conor all the time trying harder to discover the secret of invisibility. The address, as one would have expected, was superb and held the audience spellbound.

131

Then it happened. A shriek came from somewhere in the midst of the closely packed crowd. Figures started weaving about, crashing into one another, and confusion reigned.

'Let me out of here,' came the cry. 'Piffle, piffle, I don't want to listen to such a lot of rubbish.'

A stick waved above the heads every now and again and a sea of startled bodies parted, revealing an irate miniature Moses in the form of Langtry Lynas. Out of the door he marched, stick at the ready for whatever unfortunate might oppose him in Donegall Place.

Despite the quality of the opening address, I am sure Conor quite possibly agreed with Langtry, uncomfortable as he always felt whilst praise was being heaped upon him.

The strong contrast between Conor and McKelvey was only equalled by that between Colin Middleton and John Luke. Luke could have been likened to McKelvey in that he dressed nearer to the businessman image than to Bohemian informality. Colin had the arty look, with his woolly polo-necked sweaters and baggy trousers. His curly mop of grey hair and strongly defined features always reminded me of Harpo Marx. The first time I met him was in an office behind Belfast City Hall when he was working as a damask designer. The meticulous demands of such design-ing must have had a great influence on his painting style, particularly in his early works that are so reminiscent of Dali. Then he was always sur-rounded by doodles, tiny pencil drawings so precise and so beautifully drawn that you could not help but be fascinated. You could see from them that his interests and ambitions lay far beyond damask designing. When he deserted the industrial scene, I believe it lost less than the world of art gained, a supremely imaginative artist with a facile brush and an incredible colour sense. Colin never rested, but he kept experimen-ting with different styles throughout his life, in pursuit of perfection. His output was colossal yet he was never uninteresting; each phase he passed through had its own magic and I enjoyed everything he did, yet I could never forget those first tiny Middleton doodles I saw on the squared paper of the damask designer.

John Luke had a long angular face, was thin of hair and had skin so clear as to be almost transparent. His cheeks had a delicate pink hue and his remarkably large eyes reflected his kindly disposition. Given to wear-ing white shirts with long stiffly laundered collars, he knotted his tie so neatly that it looked like a clip-on. John must have had the longest fingers of any artist I knew and no one can dispute the fact that he made good use of them. He was obsessed with glazes and the old masters' approach to painting. Indeed, John took as long to paint a picture as did the old masters he so much admired. Some would have it that his meticulous approach made for frozen action in his figure painting, but the rhythmical movement and translucent colour he achieved in his landscapes made him a modern master. His mural in Belfast City Hall must surely be one of the greatest in the British Isles or beyond and undoubtedly the most undervalued.

I do not know what he was like as a teacher, but he was certainly unstinting in sharing his knowledge with his friends. In this way, those of us who grew to know him intimately were more fortunate than we could have realised at the time.

I can still see Stanley Spencer standing at the door of Keelong, where I still lived, or, even more dramatically, at the corner of Donegall Square West, waiting for the traffic lights to change. That small figure, with an umbrella that nearly reached his chin, looked isolated against a moving backdrop of figures, all of whom seemed to tower over him, like humans over a leprechaun. He had iron-grey hair with that characteristic donkey fringe, the wire-framed glasses sitting far down his nose, and a long grey scarf flung round his neck. Each end hung down over his dark overcoat, the fringes not far from the ground. He was one of Britain's greatest painters, yet like Toulouse-Lautrec he would not be seen in a crowd. A small powerhouse of creativity, intense, enthusiastic, energetic, he could keep you enthralled for hours. He visited us often when making his periodic trips to Belfast to see his brother Harold and his niece Daphne. Daphne worked in the BBC and was married to Johnny Robinson, who ran the BBC's information department. It was through Daphne and Johnny that I got to know Stanley. Daphne's father Harold was a talented musician and he sometimes played the piano at studio evenings in the academy's rooms in the Old Museum. Harold and Stanley could almost have passed for twins: Harold the musician and Stanley the artist, sharing between them a wealth of talent.

One of the greatest sins committed by me must surely have been with regard to Stanley. He wrote me a long letter, four quarto pages of close writing, in which he invited me to his home village of Cookham for a spell. With the letter he sent me a Penguin book of his work, which he had signed. Apart from the invitation to Cookham, which naturally enough did not extend to more than a few sentences, Stanley wrote a most flattering tribute to my draughtsmanship. He analysed, criticised and eulogised. He told me to treasure my abilities and appreciate the opportunities that lay before me. It was a scholarly letter, written with as much detail and precision as he applied to his pictures. When I received the letter and the invitation, my neurosis was acting up and I could not countenance a trip to Cookham. That was my great loss, but the real sin was my cavalier attitude to the letter. I suppose, whilst it was most constructive, the flattery content embarrassed me a little. I kept it in the Penguin book. On reflection, both should have been safely lodged in a bank's safe, but one never places such mercenary values on relationships. The real values are the memories of that friendship. In a house move many years later, book and letter vanished. To this day mystery shrouds their whereabouts.

My image of Cookham, which stemmed from Spencer's paintings, was of grey stone walls running higgledy-piggledy, one through the other like a stone maze; a patchwork quilt of small overgrown lots, heavy with weeds, all contained within the eccentric grey walls; here and there a twisted rusty gate barring the passage to strangers; narrow lanes, stone- and gravel-strewn, and tiny crowded graveyards with ivy and wild roses abounding, exuberant in the gardens of death; ancient tombstones aslant in drunken disorder, like rotten teeth in a witch's mouth; a place waiting for the sun to break through, waiting patiently for the Spencerian resurrection. While Stanley Spencer created a somewhat morbid impression on me, at the same time I could always, rightly or wrongly, extract a feeling of macabre humour from those images. I am sure cartoonist Charles Addams would have appreciated this small, eccentric genius, wheeling a battered pram full of working materials along those laneways lined with sombre high walls.

17

POETS AND PEASANTS

I CAN RECALL WITH A WRY SMILE an amusing incident on one visit to
Campbell's coffee house, that haunt of intellectuals – novelists,
actors, artists, playwrights, poets and poseurs. Even when absent, I
was always there dominating the scene through the murals Alfred
Campbell had commissioned me to paint. It would be nice to think that
it was that backdrop which attracted the clientele of celebrities. On this
occasion I was to meet two friends for coffee, Billy Millar (later the
film star Stephen Boyd) and Lawrence Beatty, who, years afterwards, by
sheer coincidence, was to have a cousin of mine as his stepmother.
When I arrived they were sitting listening to a person with whom I was
unacquainted. The said stranger was regaling the pair with a Jewish joke.
It is claimed by many that I have a somewhat Jewish cast of features, so
my appearance on the scene at that precise moment was catastrophic.
The stranger stopped dead in the middle of his flow. This he probably
would have done anyway in acknowledgement of the arrival of a new-
comer. However, this stoppage was different, it being accompanied by
a look of alarm and a mild glow of pink to the cheeks. I realised he must
have imagined that I was a rabbi or, at the very least, a cantor.

On reflection, I do not think I reacted as a nice person should to his
obvious discomfiture. I spread both my hands in Yiddish fashion and
said, 'Why don't you finish the joke already?'

He did not, and would not, and Billy and Lawrence laughed harder
than they would have done had his tag line been delivered.

My late cousin Peter Bew was the victim of another humorous yet
embarrassing incident in that coffee house. He was sitting chatting to
three rather attractive females, doing his best to impress. Things were
going splendidly and he had their undivided attention, which turned out

135

to be the worst thing that could have happened. He took a large bite out of a bun and set it down on his plate. His charm façade shattered at the horrific sight of four wired teeth gleaming back at him from the bun. I imagine that the three lovelies were too lady-like to laugh at the time, but I also can assume that they were less inhibited once they got outside Campbell's door in Donegall Square.

The poet John Hewitt's was the place to meet people. They homed in on number 18, Mountcharles, like bees to a hive. From near and far they came – young men and women with aspirations, the famous, the would-bes, and the never-would-bes. A tossed salad of poets, writers, artists, critics and raconteurs was always on the menu. John would be in the chair, as always, and even when not in voice, his was the omni-presence – or was it his devoted wife Roberta (Ruby to us) who should have claimed the title?

The first time I visited John and Ruby was with Ian, and they were then living at Cliftonville. The only people there on that particular evening were the Friers boys and the solicitor and poet Roy McFadden. Roy sat on the floor by the fireside, his arms hugging his knees and his gaze directed to the flames. He did not talk a lot that night, nor did we, but John was virtually Falstaffian. There were times when he could be very overbearing, insulting, pedantic, and other times when he was dis-tant. His father, whom I knew when he was a member of the Ulster Academy of Arts Association, had an aloof bearing and could have passed as an older version of the son. Despite this inherent trait, I always had the feeling that both men were naturally shy behind their outward ap-pearances of superiority.

Ian, always an incorrigible leg-puller, had one of his biggest catches at John Hewitt's flat in Mountcharles. It was one deeply meaningful evening, and an all-impressive cell of intellectuals was assembled to-gether in his, John Hewitt's, name and the conversation plodded from impressionists to regional poets. Regionalism was, of course, one of John's pet subjects at the time so the discourse got deeper and deeper. The master threw himself into this his favourite arena and soon it all be-gan to get, I suspect, a little too heavy for my big brother. The moment a break came in the conversation, the irrepressible jester struck.

'John, being an expert on regionalism and poetry in general, you would be acquainted with Gaelic poets?' he asked, his face deadly serious.

136

Sam Hanna Bell (left)
and John Hewitt (right)

'We-e-ll, to a certain degree, although not, of course, a Gaelic speaker' came the answer.

'Have you ever heard of the great Pachal O'Keagh?' queried Ian, seriously innocent.

There was silence as the assembled brains, in conjunction with the master's, groped in the darkness of total ignorance. Someone dared to titter. And then it happened. Spontaneous combustion – the room rocked with mirth, and no one laughed more than John, who shook like a jelly on a vibrator. Those Mountcharles gatherings were always interesting, with John in his element and his wife Ruby standing by, the pride in her husband shining from her eyes.

I first met Sam Hanna Bell at the Hewitts' flat. There were many characters there, but only one stuck out that night in my eyes. Perhaps it was because this was my first sighting of Sam, but I still think it was because of the fact he was seated lower then everyone else. He was on a stool and I thought, That's a big man, he must be about six foot six, at least. He had a towering brow, with fair, bushy eyebrows pulled

137

down, throwing his piercing blue eyes into shadow. A large romanesque nose hung over and dominated a straw-coloured moustache, an exact match of his eyebrows. All this was set off by a very large and very determined-looking chin. Every now and then he would twitch his nose, close his eyes and thrust his chin forward – a nervous habit that served only to emphasise or draw attention to the strength of his face. Huge hands rested on his knees and these, too, added to the impression of a really big man. When he stood up, he shrunk to being an average-sized person with above-average head and hands. The head was an essential for the brain he had, and the hands he certainly put to good use. Sam launched me into radio drama in a couple of his productions about a character called Jimmy Gimme. He had me play about five characters in each presentation, much to the chagrin of some of the cast, who were Equity members, but were not, as Sam observed, 'mimics'.

The night I first met Roy McFadden at the Hewitts' Cliftonville home was the beginning of a very long friendship. He was young then when he sat in front of the fire, posed like the boy Raleigh, and a lot of living lay ahead of us. Roy, with Barbara Hunter, set up a publishing business. (Well, you could not call it a business because it made no money – it consumed it.) The Lisnagarvey Press published my first book, *Wholly Friers*, in 1948. It contained fifty-three cartoons and a foreword by John Hewitt, all for the price of three shillings and sixpence. At the price it was a best-seller – not a profit-maker, just a best-seller. Not to be deterred, the duo produced a magazine, *Rann*, for which I designed many covers. There was never any mention of money; we did it for love and to encourage the arts. You could rightly claim Roy and Barbara to have been trailblazers for the arts council. Roy is the proud possessor of three of my oil paintings and a pencil drawing – well, I do not really know whether he is proud or not, but I am that he has them, and better still, he did purchase them.

A strong love affair builds up between an artist and some of his pictures: not all of them, just some, and of those, some deeper than others, as with people. In the case of other pictures, again like people, you would care little if you never saw them again. Once you have parted with them, a sadness remains, as at the end of a passionate affair. Many go, never to be seen again, leaving you only with memories. Paintings into which you have put so much love, enjoyment, excitement and deep feeling become so much a part of you that it is like losing a limb.

138

Temptation in the Wilderness (Courtesy of RUA)

When you are fortunate enough to see one of your paintings many years later, the experience can shoot you back through time so excitingly that you can almost smell the freshly applied paint. This was the case when I recently renewed my acquaintance with those in Roy McFadden's collection. A pencil drawing, which depicts the twelve apostles, was interesting – fine silver point heads, each about three-quarters of an inch, were formalised and decorative in style. This work was done in a period when I had an ambition to paint the Stations of the Cross; unhappily, I was never approached by the Catholic Church and, who knows, maybe another Michelangelo was lost to the world. However, the Royal Ulster Academy benefited, as did my friends, and the founders of the Lyric Theatre, Pearse and Mary O'Malley, from this period. The academy got my *Temptation in the Wilderness* for their diploma collection, and Pearse and Mary have *Nativity*, which presently hangs in the Mater Hospital.

My painting output naturally suffered through the insatiable appetites of the media and publishing houses. The theatre design world also took its toll of my studio time. Though my output could never be described as prolific, my first one-man show in the CEMA gallery in Donegall

139

Place in October 1953 had eighty-four exhibits: twenty oil paintings and the remainder drawings and illustrations. The foreword to my catalogue was written by John Hewitt, and his summation of the artist is worth reprinting here. As keeper of the art at the Belfast Museum and Art Gallery, he was the authority, and his advice was much valued. To have him write a foreword was a great compliment.

My first one-man show, at the CEMA gallery, Donegall Place, October 1953; *left to right:* Nelson Browne, myself and John Hewitt (Courtesy of *Belfast News-Letter*)

Although this is his first one-man exhibition, Rowel Friers has, in the past decade, shown his work regularly with the Royal Hibernian and Royal Ulster Academies, and several of his canvases have been acquired by the Haverty Trust and CEMA. He is also one of the small band of Northern artists who have been represented in exhibitions of Irish painting touring in Great Britain.

Surely the most versatile of his generation here, he has produced a steady flow of book illustrations, book-plates, caricatures and cartoons as well as oil paintings; and in design his interest has ranged from Christmas cards to stage sets. His humorous drawings in black and white have been contributed to the leading journals in these islands and by their authority he has clearly joined that select group of which George Morrow, David Wilson and Matt Sanford have been our best known representatives.

Busy with so many things, painting has necessarily been less his profession than his indulgence, but here too the same consistency of craftsmanship apparent elsewhere is maintained; for, disciplined by the techniques

140

of pictorial reproduction and block making, he has learned by rigorous practice to give his work in any medium the effect of swiftness and economy of means and of assurance in handling. In the physical manipulation of pigment he stands with John Luke, with Neville Johnson and with the Colin Middleton of ten years ago, rather than with the majority of his less dextrous contemporaries.

That the geniality of observation evident in his cartoons springs from temperament rather than from deliberate effort is clearly demonstrated by such paintings as *The Fair Day*, *The Variety Market*, *The Big Drum*, and *The Brawl*: but that his interest is not limited to this mode can also be shown by religious paintings like *Nativity*, imaginative paintings like *The Blasted Heath*, by portraits like that of R.H. McCandless, the actor.

John chaired the opening and his fellow poet Roy McFadden was to perform the actual ceremony but the latter's sudden indisposition necessitated that my good friend from art college days, Nelson Browne, had to fill the breach. The exhibition ran from 19 October to 31 October, and was to have one visitor per minute throughout its run – an unprecedented success.

The last time I saw John was one day a few years ago when I thought I would have a peep into the Chalet d'Or. There was no point in looking for company, for the shadow cabinet had dissolved, the grim reaper and senility having seen to that. I was anxious to see what changes had been made to the interior layout; it was as it had been, but the table two-thirds of the way down on the left of the café was empty. Faces from the past flashed through my mind, as happens to a drowning man: Conor, Vitty, Ireland, Hanna Bell, Doc Ryan, Tomelty, Padraic Woods, and Johnny. Meeting closed. I did not have a quorum.

As I turned to leave, I spotted him. Sitting on the right-hand side of the glass partition that ran the length of the premises, there he was, John Hewitt, seated at the table. Alone. His hands were placed one upon the other on top of his walking stick, his pipe sitting in the ashtray, his eyes drooped as though he were dozing. Alone, the last of that coffee set which was born round the corner in Campbell's. I was delighted to find him there, and hurried round to join him. We sat and talked for more than an hour, and I walked round with him to his bus for Balmoral and Stockman's Lane. That was in 1987 and it was the last time I saw Johnny.

18

SOLITARY CONFINEMENT

TOMORROW WILL BE DIFFERENT, I thought. Nothing can last for ever. The worst of nightmares can barely be remembered after waking. This was the logic that echoed and re-echoed through the black labyrinths of my mind and it was the one light I had, like a guttering candle flame in a draughty cell, the cell door I had slammed on the world when I committed myself to solitary confinement. No visitors were made welcome, because no visitor could make contact or communicate in any way. The hearty, well-meaning fools who would assure me there was nothing wrong, and insist that all I needed was to 'pull myself together' were a major menace. Little did they realise how closely they courted physical attack. Then there were the long-faced sympathetic Samaritans who had never experienced the condition personally but knew someone who had, and how that poor family was so worried for the months and months it took until their friend eventually got better.

It had all happened so suddenly. It was 1944, the end of the war years. Simple overwork, the doctor had said, and recommended a complete change of environment. For a couple of months I had been sitting in the same chair, looking into space, and never venturing outside the house. When the radio was playing it annoyed me, but it was too far out of my reach for me to switch it off. When on a rare occasion I could muster the mental control to walk the long mile to turn the switch, I then could not bear the silence created. Sleeplessness came at night or, at best, fitful dozing accompanied by melancholic fantasising. Once, I drifted out of such a doze to a room blue-lit by a full moon, the window frame casting the shadow of a cross on the bed-cover. My hands were placed across my chest as in everlasting repose. The morbid fancy that I was dead and lying in state made my diaphragm contract and a cold sweat break on my brow. On these occasions the most familiar surroundings changed fractionally and became entirely alien.

Cambridge was working with the civil service near London in those days. It was thought that the big city would be a sufficient change for me from the rural lethargy that was Dundonald. Considering that outside my own door lay nothing but fear for me, it was hardly surprising that London did not prove to be an instant panacea. That city, with its perpetual processions of stony-faced commuters scurrying to and fro in their workaday world like hamsters on a treadmill, was menacing to me. People in cars being perpetually stuck in traffic snarl-ups and pumping their horns in unison, impatience and short tempers being the order of the day, terrified me. Large red buses bore down on me from every conceivable angle, with giant eyes glaring. The eyes were posters advertising a magazine of the day called *Picture Post*. Eyes staring wide in which I saw madness.

Underground, the Tube resembled the interior of a bustling ant hill, with escalators and platforms packed with the living dead, automatons, each programmed towards some vital goal and time running out. That ghastly rush of air which is constant and exclusive to tubes had my hair on end and the whine and clatter of the tubes themselves, as they hurtled through the black tunnels, froze me in terror. When a tube stopped, I would be carried into it on the moving wave of humanity. Expressionless faces were everywhere: the strap-hangers, those who were buried in newspapers, and the ones who stared in a hypnotic trance at the diagrammatic map of the Underground, searching for their particular point of disembarkation.

All the theatres I attended at that time seemed geared to be unsettling, from *The Duchess of Malfi* in the Haymarket, to a Grand Guignol performance at Walham Green. Everything appeared to be aimed at driving me deeper into a world of darkness. On a visit to Chessington Zoo, much depleted because of the then wartime measures, I observed a run labelled 'leopard', and to my mental discomfort a terrier dog came running out of the sleeping quarters, barking ferociously at me. When you are not at your best of mental health, it is no comfort to see a terrier where there is supposed to be a leopard. However, my sanity was reprieved when a few seconds later a leopard appeared, stretched itself and, giving a large yawn, looked at me with a bored air and returned to its sleeping quarters closely followed by his friend, the terrier.

Then, to me, London was a nightmare, and although I was only away for three weeks, time seemed to stand still, and each day was more hideous than the previous one. How glad I was to get home, to sit in my chair again and close the cell door more firmly, if possible. However, that was not to be.

My mother asked me if I was feeling better. I lied and said, 'Yes, of course.'

Mothers are not easily fooled, so she used a ploy she knew would test me to the full. 'Will you go for eggs for me?' she asked.

My whole inner being froze. I knew she was trying me out, and to convince her, or minimise her concern, I must make an effort. To get the eggs meant a half-mile walk ALONE. It also meant going out into that weird vacuum with moving things called people, who did not relate to my life – or, more correctly, I did not relate to theirs. I was alone in my cell and could never come out of it. Inside the house my cell felt impregnable, but outside something threatened, something I could never define, intangible, inexplicable, and wholly terrifying. Now I had to make a decision. 'Yes, of course I'll go,' I said. That decision was the most courageous and most vital I have ever made.

It was the longest half-mile I have ever walked, and that day was the stillest I have ever experienced. People walked past as in slow motion, and cars whizzed past in silence. Only the drumming of my temples and the thump of my heart were audible to me, and they were deafening. Perspiration streamed down the sides of my face, and my shirt collar was cold, limp and wet as it rubbed on my neck. I felt my back itch with the motion of flowing rivulets. My trousers stuck to my legs as though I had walked through a stream. Always I thought of turning back. I wanted desperately to give up and race home again. My body was reluctantly moving forward, while my mind was fighting its own battle: Don't weaken, you can make it – It's impossible, I'm frightened – Be stronger. Fight it. You must win. You can't torture your family any more.

On and on went the fight, and on and on the walk, for ever and ever, strife without end. Then, suddenly, the doorway, the woman and the eggs. I had made it all on my own.

That was my first mental breakdown. It had lasted the most of two years, and it was overcome by personal determination. Triumphant in victory, I vowed that I would never let it happen again. Sadly, vows are not immune to pressures.

144

19

ANOTHER STAGE IN ART

IT WAS FRANK McKELVEY JUNIOR who was responsible for my
Thespian activities and thus, indeed, was indirectly a contributor
to my eventual married bliss. Because Frank and his then girlfriend
Alma wanted to join a dramatic club, I was inveigled by them into joining Fisherwick Dramatic Society. After about three weeks my friends
found the drama of life and realism more compelling and made their
exits, leaving me to 'strut and fret my hour upon the stage' alone. In
retrospect I owe them a lot, because it was there I found confidence and
love. Love of the theatre was born in me, and in Fisherwick it flourished. There too I found my own leading lady, Yvonne. We married
and produced our own cast of one daughter and two sons.

Before the lure of amateur dramatics, I was already an ardent theatre-
goer and had many friends in the 'legitimate theatre', as it is called. Pro-
fessionals must, by implication, look upon amateurs as illegitimates.
When I joined Fisherwick, I had no ambitions whatsoever either to
'strut' or to 'fret'. Indeed, the thought of actually going on stage chilled
me to the marrow. At that time in my life if, in the Royal Ulster
Academy, I was asked merely to second a vote of thanks, my innards
became a butterfly farm. Most people laugh in my face when I tell them
this, they cannot believe I was ever shy. However, it is a fact. I had a
very retiring personality, and hated the direct gaze of enquiring eyes. My
tongue would go dry and seize up, and my face aspire to pillar-box red,
the spotlight made me feel I was, or should be, on the run. Fisherwick
dispelled all those inhibitions that go to make one a jellyfish.

On my first night in Adelaide Street, the drama group's meeting
place, I informed Sidney Hewitt, producer, and the then drama adviser
to CEMA, that in no way would I countenance acting, but would be

interested in stage design. 'Good', was his answer. 'We shall see.' We did see, and within four meetings I was designing the set for a Welsh comedy, *Wishing Well* by Eynon Evans, and rehearsing the part of a Welsh chauffeur. It was a biggish part and for a reluctant beginner had all the enormity of tackling Lear.

Designing the set and painting it was fun, and it was also my first-ever stage design. As I worked I muttered, and some of the group members no doubt thought me a little eccentric. I was muttering like a priest over his breviary, memorising my lines and praying that my memory would hold out come the first night. Happily, I was always a reasonably good mimic, and the Welsh accent seemed to help my confidence, possibly because it masked my own. The masks of drama mean a lot to me – strange dialects, greasepaint and crêpe hair – things to hide behind, like the sofa I hid behind as a child, drawing our visitors. I really grew to love acting. It was like an extension of my caricaturing, living the characters I drew, drawing live pictures on the stage.

We performed *Wishing Well* about ten or twelve times, including a week in the Little Theatre, Bangor. It was one of Sidney Hewitt's many successful productions. He was a thorough producer, verging on the martinet, sticking rigidly to the directions as per the book. You could never have said he had any great flairs of imagination; the frills he left to the actors, those who might have any. Sidney was an expert at pace, insisting that you should not expect a cue word, but pre-empt it where feasible, have the dialogue flow as in normal conversation. This policy meant that performers had to know the play thoroughly and not just their own lines – a frequent failing with amateur companies.

During the Bangor run of *Wishing Well*, Sidney was suffering from an ear infection, which necessitated his head being swathed in bandages like a mummy. He also suffered the extreme hospitality of the Bangor drama folk, who swelled his head with praise to such an extent that his bandages were under severe strain. The liquor doled out to him did not help. He developed, through over-indulgence, a sense of insecurity and got very fussy indeed about pace, audience reaction, and how the play was going. Having had countless rehearsals and about five live shows we, the cast, were enjoying the run. One particular night in Bangor remains recorded in my mind for ever. Sidney had got himself on overload, deserted his drinking buddies and made a most determined, although somewhat unsteady, way backstage. On stage, a very sober and

well-versed cast was enjoying a smooth performance before a most
appreciative audience. A loud prompt shot across the stage like an arrow,
emanating from the window stage right, and into the wings, where a
baffled prompter dropped his script in shock. The performers jumped
visibly but carried on. No one had dried but someone had definitely
blundered. Then, horror of horrors, another prompt, this time from
behind the stairs back centre, sailed low and clear over the astounded
heads of our rapt audience. Then it started, arrows in every direction,
as the tempo of on-stage dialogue accelerated. I thought I recognised
that voice, despite the slurring, and as I moved across the stage to the
settle, where we were to do a three-hander, with me doing a long solilo-
quy, I realised it was Sydney.

I took my seat beside the other two and, crossing my leg nonchalantly, or as nonchalantly as I could in the circumstances, I stubbed out
the cigarette I had been smoking and casually turned to throw it on the
fire. For a fraction of a second, which seemed like three or four minutes,
my arm froze in mid-air. My expression, I know, would have convinced
the audience that I had either dried or the play was about to take a more
melodramatic turn. For the three of us on that settle, it certainly did. Sitting in the firelight glow, indeed resting on the coals, was the mummy's
head jabbering away. Few, if any, of the audience could have had a clear
view of the ghastly spectacle – pure Grand Guignol. We continued only
slightly daunted or, so we hoped, gave the appearance of that. The head
disappeared as fast as it had arrived, and miraculously reappeared complete with body behind our settle, prompting, prompting, prompting.

The three of us, in a desperate attempt to drown the drunken prompts, started raising our octaves. This had the effect of creating something more akin to a bar-room brawl than a civil conversation. The act ended to sporadic applause and an errant producer being hastily escorted back to his saboteurs at the bar.

With Sidney Hewitt, postmortems were always demoralising. Only the new boy or girl gave a good performance, putting the rest of us to shame. They had shown talent, attack and enough charisma to lift the whole play from complete disaster. How remarkable it was that each new boy (and girl) was so consistent! They only ever gave one sustained performance and that was on their debut. This was how he kept us on a tight rein. We worked hard to please him but we never succeeded, even though we proved ourselves to be the best team around at that time. Indeed, remembering all those people who were with Fisherwick, and the talents they displayed, I feel they would still be top-leaguers today.

I have remained an ardent theatre-goer and consider drama at its best to be one of the great art forms. Nothing else can so directly entertain and at the same time educate. Should you be fortunate enough to become involved in a good drama club and become an actor–member, your self-confidence will grow, as will your circle of friends. It is both exciting and creative and, indeed, addictive. In my own association with the amateur stage I learned a great deal about the intricacies of stage design, which was to prove most useful in later years when designing for the professional theatre. The acting itself gave me an assurance I would never have attained otherwise, and for that I am eternally grateful.

During those amateur days Yvonne and I had much advice from that wonderful old man of the theatre, R.H. McCandless. After we were married he stayed with Yvonne and myself on many weekends, and when he was not playing with our children he would regale us with stories of his early days when he created a home-made theatre with his brother. Later he would tell us about his work with the Ballycarry Players, about their successes and catastrophes, all the fun and the failures; how butterflies in the tummy ensured a sense of responsibility and if you did not have any, then disaster could result. He emphasised the importance of the timing of dialogue and of avoiding character assassination by over-playing.

We learned a great deal from that wise and delightful old friend. He had turned his back on pharmaceuticals, for which he was fully qualified, to give his all to acting. His contribution to the Northern Ireland stage was great, and his professional guidance was generously given to young actors like Colin Blakely, Stephen Boyd and James Ellis. His devotion to the stage and in particular to Ulster plays was quite exceptional. A keen observer of the local scene, he had much in common with William Conor, and if ever two men were worthy of knighthoods, they were, for their enormous contribution to the arts in Ulster.

20

DARK OF THE MOON

WHEN, IN THE MID-1950S, through the pressure of a very heavy workload, I had a second mental breakdown, my cousin Dr Kenneth Bew recommended I consult Dr Pearse O'Malley. Having beaten that condition first time round through sheer determination, I was under the misapprehension that it would never return. How wrong I was. And how much worse it is the second time, when that feeling of utter defeat envelops you. I am called upon to talk about it from time to time, and it is not the easiest of conditions to describe. The only comfort you can derive from such a malady is the proof positive that there is something between your ears that can go wrong.

The best way I can effectively describe that state of mind is to liken it to being in an empty theatre. Imagine, if you will, that you are seated in a massive theatre that has no audience, just rows and rows of seats, all empty. You, and you alone, are the audience, sitting in complete isolation on a seat at the very back, enveloped in darkness. The only lighting comes from a narrow slit in the distance. This area is brilliantly lit: it is the stage. On that stage a play is in progress, a heavy, complex drama entitled Life. Your ears can only take in an occasional word. The rest is merely noise as far as you are concerned. Your concentration is nil. All you are conscious of is the pitch darkness that enshrouds you. The performers, all animation and incoherent chatter, fill you with an inexplicable fear. Your solar plexus grips madly. A desperate urge possesses you to flee from it all, and you look despairingly around for an exit sign. But no such sign exists in that well of darkness. A terrifying loneliness holds you trapped with a performance which is nightmarish. It is a play in which something tells you you belong, but you cannot enter. Your script has gone. You just sit in the darkness of your own mind, hoping that someone, somewhere, will open a door leading to light and reason, so that you may escape this morbid theatre of your imaginings.

Pearse O'Malley proved to be all my cousin had claimed him to be, kind and most sympathetic. My first appointment was at his surgery in Derryvolgie Avenue, where he put me through the routine physical checks, followed by question time. Further appointments were made at his clinic in the Mater Hospital, where I had electroconvulsive therapy. One of the most frustrating aspects of this routine was the jolly anaesthetist, Dr John Cooper. He would start to tell you a funny story and, just as he was about to give you the punch line, your lights went out. When you woke again you could not even remember the joke in order to try imagining what the punch line might have been. Pearse O'Malley's treatment was a pretty rapid road to complete recovery. It was also an even more rapid road back to Derryvolgie Avenue, where he and his wife Mary then ran the Lyric Theatre in their own home. I became one of their main set designers.

Mary O'Malley might not have been able to draw blood from a stone, but she sure as hell would be able to find some constructive use for the stone. A small, formidable woman, obsessed with what appeared to be an impossible dream, she could talk you into anything. She knew what she wanted and she invariably got it. The monument to her single-mindedness is Belfast's Lyric Theatre. Her way was fraught with obstacles, but a tornado like Mary is unstoppable.

My association with the O'Malleys was always a happy one, even in my darkest hours with Pearse, who was always gentle, and so competent and understanding that you valued the strength his friendship gave. Mary could charm anything out of you, even the impossible, for example, a set for *Peer Gynt* on the Derryvolgie stage, designed and painted in a weekend. That stage was not much larger than a dining table to seat twelve, with two of the twelve at each end. Productions on that table top would have challenged theatres with the most sophisticated of staging facilities. *Volpone, Under Milk Wood* and *The Heart's a Wonder* provided just a few of the designer's problems. Later, when the new Lyric Theatre was opened in Ridgeway Street in 1968, it was like moving from a hot-press to a banqueting room – space, glorious space. There we had *Juno and the Paycock, The Becauseway,* and my favourite, *Luther,* plus countless others which only Mary could dream up.

151

With her strong will and artistic single-mindedness, Mary was an irresistible force. Many were in awe of her and few there were who would take liberties. I was fortunate in that I could wisecrack with her without incurring grievous bodily harm. Once we were at the back of Derryvolgie packing a set I had designed for *The Heart's a Wonder*. Everyone else was milling around getting the flats ready for a Scottish tour. Mary was overseer. As I stood beside her, my eyes wandered up to the chimney of her live-in theatre. An elaborate piece of contemporary sculpture was affixed to that chimney. Television had been installed and the aerial was a contorted piece of ironwork.

'Do you watch TV much?' I asked idly.

Her answer was instant and, still keeping her eyes on the packing process, she replied, 'No, I will only watch it when we get our own national station.' Mary was, and still is, a fervent nationalist.

I looked again at that aerial and said: 'Well, dammit, with that aerial you should get the Vatican direct!'

She laughed, as she always could.

Once, I remember taking the doyen of Ulster actors, R.H. McCandless, a man who never minced his words and was often given to the sardonic, to see T.S. Eliot's *The Family Reunion* at Derryvolgie. The place was packed, and from curtain-up R.H. started to grumble because he did not like the play. His grumble was as loud as the performers' projections and I felt both uncomfortable and uneasy.

'Do they understand what they are saying?' he asked me. This was a criticism of the actors' reading of the play.

'If they don't understand what they're saying,' he continued, 'how the hell do they expect us to understand?'

That was truly an uncomfortable night for me, but all was not over. After the performance I introduced him to Mary.

'What did you think of the performance?' she asked.

'W-e-ll, I suppose,' he said, reaching out a massive hand to hers, 'w-e-ll, I suppose I've got to congratulate you on your courage, anyway.'

I agreed with him, as I did not like the play either, and there are very few alive with Mary's courage.

21

THE BIG DAY

FISHERWICK, AS I HAVE SAID, gave me confidence, and it also gave me sufficient courage to ask Yvonne to be my wife. Fortunately for me, the dramatic society had also given her enough courage to accept. Our romance was strictly offstage, so much so that the players had no idea we were anything other than 'just good friends'. Neither of us ever wanted it any other way and the 'greatest moment of drama' Fisherwick must ever have experienced was when they heard the announcement of our marriage, for 27 August 1954.

I was struggling with the grey piece of material, that hybrid between a bra and a waistcoat which is part and parcel of morning wear, that infuriating piece of male attire that can be as frustrating to a nervous groom as erecting a deck chair would be to a man with ten thumbs. My two brothers had already mastered the situation and were swanning about like a couple of successful financiers, completely oblivious of my gyrations. As the latter-day Valentino, Ian was completely at home in the formal trappings – he swaggered. Bill, who had protested vehemently about having to 'dress up in this bloody gear', had succumbed to pressure and was now looking even more at home despite his initial objections. Mother, also appropriately apparelled for the big day, kept looking through the window for the first sight of a wedding limousine. I was running a very poor fourth in the wedding stakes, even though I was to play the male lead.

When my car arrived, my best man Nelson Browne was in full flow. We had been friends since my art college days, when Nelson was head of English in the Belfast College of Technology. A brilliant conversationalist at the best of times, he was now excelling himself. On a rare high, he was obviously completely possessed by a sense of occasion. Cocktails of wisdom and whimsicality flowed from him as exotic blooms and fruit from a cornucopia. I was listening but not absorbing, my mind being locked in the complications of high finance. A sidelong glance showed me that Nelson's tie was a little askew. I drew attention to the flaw in his sartorial perfection and turned my head again. I gazed out at Belfast as its streets slipped past our limousine's windows. Outside it was a Northern Irish day – like its politics, very unsettled. I smiled wryly to myself at something Nelson had said. My mind, preoccupied as it was, had to go into a fast rewind to sort out the full gist of what we, or rather he, had been expounding upon. Everyone occasionally experiences such moments, when words are fed into your grey-celled computer at a time when that same computer is running on another programme; a time when you are aroused from a dream to a non-too-clear reality; a time when you snap from darkness to light, automatically switching your expression to 'intelligent interest being taken'. On such occasions you invariably take solace from the fact that most compulsive talkers are unaware that you have 'gone missing'. Without doubt, such was the case on that memorable day.

Our limousine, a Daimler, continued to glide silently and majestically along Chichester Street towards the city hall. My mind suddenly signalled to me: 'time for action'. Grabbing my grey topper and matching gloves, I slid open the glass panel at the driver's ear and asked him to stop on the corner of Donegall Square West and Wellington Place. Without question he complied. I opened the door and leaped out, just aware of the pale, bewildered, and much-alarmed face of Nelson. He made some sporadic and unintelligible hand-to-mouth signals. I turned

The wedding party; *left to right:* Joyce Hodge, William Carter, Mother, myself and Yvonne, Agnes Kidd, Nelson Browne and Aideen Hall

tails on him and fled across the highly trafficked road to a doorway at the corner of Fountain Lane. I rushed through the doorway to the foot of the time-worn and foot-weary wooden stairs. Donning my topper and striking my thigh pantomimically with my gloves, I thought, He's in for one helluva surprise, and took the stairs two at a time.

My destination was a small office run by a small publisher of a small magazine. He had a small but well-endowed secretary. Most important of all, he owed me a small sum of money over a long period of time. It was the sudden recollection of this debt that had impaired my concentration on Nelson's outpourings. The small publisher's office loomed before me. Under my impact the door fell open, as did the mouths of one small publisher and his small secretary.

'I want my fiver right away...in a desperate hurry...getting married...' I panted demandingly.

With the speed of light a wallet miraculously appeared and a shaking hand wavered in the direction of my waistcoat, a fiver limply dangling between finger and thumb. I thanked them both and made an exit as swift as my entrance. To this day I laugh at that incident and I wonder. I never saw either of them again. I cannot help thinking, did I do any damage to their nervous systems? At that time a fiver bought a great deal more than it does today – artists were selling watercolours for little more – but could I possibly have been in such dire straits? Could the wedding not have proceeded without it? Did those two just imagine my visit a sort of joint hallucination? Such questions must have gone through their heads, I feel sure, as I recall those transfixed expressions on the morning of 27 August 1954.

On my triumphant return to the Daimler I could see the light of relief come back into Nelson's eyes. Poor man, his first thought must have been that I had been taken short – which in a way you could say I had been. But then, of course, I might have been leaving him and my beautiful bride Yvonne waiting at the church. I wonder (for he never told me) how he would have dealt with such a situation had I really turned out to be a bounder. Still, it all proved my confidence in him for he would certainly have been the best man to explain it.

That day, as I say, was unsettled, as, indeed, was Nelson. Dark grey clouds floated low in the sky in small menacing groups. Periodically they would release great downpours of such ferocity that the rain ricocheted off the pavements like the silver spokes of a bicycle wheel. Just as

suddenly as the showers started, they would stop, and the sun then elbowed its way through, shining with sufficient intensity to create a slight steam on the pavements. Weatherwise we had taken a calculated risk for our wedding date, but then are not all wedding days a calculated risk?

We arrived at the church, McCracken Memorial on the Malone Road, to be met at the portals by two handsome young gentlemen, Yvonne's nephew, Gerard Gould, and my nephew, Terence Mayne.

Our wedding day, 27 August 1954, with Yvonne wearing the dress I had designed especially for her

Also in attendance and looking extremely elegant was groomsman and publisher William Carter. Nelson and I were conducted to our seats by the nephews, two most efficient ushers.

As we walked up the aisle, faces familiar and unfamiliar craned their necks to get a view of the groom and escorts. A mental image of mine suddenly transformed the scene into a courtroom crowded with spectators and me, the accused, found guilty, being directed to the cells. The sentence – life. The organ music died away. To a slow lifting movement of the reverend's hand we all rose and faced the altar, and music burst forth into the Wedding March. There was an excited though hushed babble from the assembled guests behind us. I was tempted to take a quick peek over my shoulder. The organ increased in volume as did the babble. The excitement was catching. The star of the show had arrived. I did not need to strain my neck. I knew she was beautiful and I had already seen the bridal gown. Very difficult to please, Yvonne had had to have her own exclusive designer. She wanted a creation that was for her and her alone. This did indeed turn out to be the case as many years later our daughter Vivien did not wear it at her own wedding.

Here I shall digress for a moment to consider Viv's wedding on 9 January 1982. At her ceremony I was more nervous than at my own. What sort of a man would want to give his only daughter away? It seemed so uncaring, though if it had been a case of selling her, no man could have met my reserve. Standing in the porch of St Philip and St James in Holywood with Vivien on my arm, I felt as though I were in the wings about to go on stage. Butterflies fluttered madly inside me and, like the day itself, I was very cold indeed. It was a really white wedding, the snow being about eighteen inches deep. The Trumpet Voluntary suddenly crashed up the aisle towards me, Viv gave me a tug, and we set off through that cascade of reverberating sound. Vivien is petite and at my rate of knots I doubt if her feet touched the ground very often. Afterwards she said to me: 'Dad, that was the Trumpet Voluntary, not the Post-horn Gallop. Were you so anxious to be rid of me?'

Vivien's gown was as white as the snow outside but Yvonne's was a softer shade. I quote a newspaper description of Yvonne's exclusive model: 'It was in honey-coloured figured French brocade, with a slim bodice finished with a Medici collar and a graceful skirt ending in a circular train.' The bridegroom was her exclusive designer, and the dress was painstakingly made by Eileen Riddell, wife of the late Pat Riddell

157

(UTV's answer to Gilbert Harding). She did have several more gowns by the same designer but pressure of other art forms was to prove too much and Northern Ireland lost a budding couturier.

Before our wedding I had been hospitalised with a stomach ulcer. I had a tube up my nose, drips going into my arm, and enjoyed the attentions of a few white coats who paid me the occasional visit in order to mark up their pools hanging on the end of my bed. I was told I was going into hospital for complete rest but the matron, Miss Elliott, thought that therapy was also called for. Accordingly, I was presented with brushes, paints and boards and set to work to produce posters for the ward. Pictures of nurses in hobnailed boots, noisy patients *et al.*, were created in the interest of quietude in the wards. When Florence Elliott thought it was right, it was right.

As you may imagine, my stay in hospital did not add to my confidence as a bridegroom. Supposing my ulcer volcano erupted again? How undignified it would be if I had to be stretchered home from the ceremony. Prior to the wedding I had requested that newspapers refrain from taking pictures. I was, after all, not in the pink after losing a great deal of weight. They all promised to hold back on the pics and I felt happier. Following the service, as we came out of the church we were met by what looked like lightning and two voices yelling, 'Come on, Rowel. Give us a big smile!' As newsmen have been known to do, they broke their promise; one from an English daily, the other from south of the border, were the culprits on this occasion.

I was refused medical permission to leave Northern Ireland for the honeymoon we had planned in Paris and Cornwall. The medicos dictated a home resort so we ended up first in Rostrevor and then in Dublin. On the morning after our wedding, a member of the hotel staff proudly presented us with a copy of the *Daily Mail*. The headline on the front page announced: 'Groom has to eat chicken at his wedding'. This was supported by a photograph on church steps of a smiling bride propping up what appeared to be a stick (or sick) insect in a morning suit. If you are known at all and there is a story attached to you, then you are meat for the media. So Paris and Cornwall became Dublin and Rostrevor, but we have lived happily ever after despite that minor setback.

22

STARS IN MY EYES

WHEN BILLY MILLAR HAD BEEN discovered by Michael Redgrave (who had spotted Billy as a handsome commissionaire manning a cinema door in London), and made the silver screen as Stephen Boyd in *The Man Who Never Was*, I thought that would be the last we would see of him. I was convinced he would make it to Hollywood. However, it was not to be as I had imagined. An opportunity to see him again arose when he was making the film *Seven Waves Away* at Shepperton Studios in London. I happened to be in London and before going had been given 'Stephen Boyd's' phone number by the inimitable J.G. Devlin. 'Pull the bugger's leg, Rowley,' he said. J.G. always referred to me as Rowley Freers, despite the fact that he knew the proper pronunciation perfectly well. There has always been, and probably always will be, much difficulty with my name, and J.G. played on this to send me up. 'Rowel' is pronounced as in 'towel', 'vowel', and 'bowel', and 'Friers' as in monasteries.

Armed with the phone number and J.G.'s encouragement, I rang Stephen's flat, assuming another voice, very broad and very coarse. When he answered, I started with that most irritating of openings, 'You know who this is?'

'I've no idea. Who is it?' he replied.

'Come, nye, ye know rightly. I hope you're nat gettin' a big head?'

'Who is it?' – with the slightest edge to his tone.

I kept baiting him for quite a time. I even suggested that I might call with him if he was likely to be having a house party with some of his film star friends; and all this in the voice and character of someone you would not want to know. It says a lot for Stephen's good nature that he did not hang up on me.

At last I said, 'You know well who it is – it's Rowel!'

A few choice and very rare titles were readily conferred upon me. He laughed heartily and arranged to meet me the following day. That arrangement was to prove both exciting and educational, for Stephen had rightly imagined I might like to visit the studios where he was working on *Seven Waves Away*. The studios were as active as an ant hill, with people travelling in all directions, some fast, some slow, and all with purpose. There were lines of caravans, huts and large constructions resembling aircraft hangars. Familiar faces loomed before me and vanished before I could recall their names. Faces of actors and actresses who appeared in film after film, but were never stars, faces with which you would be so familiar that they were tantamount to being personal friends; these were the working actors, or those essential characters without whom a film would be incomplete.

We made our way to one of the hangars which was the studio in which they were shooting *Seven Waves Away*. It had a high roof, spider-webbed with iron girders, from which were suspended lights of every shape and size. There were cameras on wheels, booms and hand-held. Cables twisted hither and thither, and technicians fussed around checking and rechecking the setting-up. Stephen left to get ready for his scene and I was alone in an atmosphere of chattering activity.

Before me, taking up most of the huge studio, was a massive tank of water. At the furthermost end of the tank about one-third of the surface was covered with a clear plastic that created a strange illusion of distance. From the back of the tank a large white cyclorama curved gently upwards towards the roof; a lifeboat floated lazily in the forefront of the tank. A number of actors arrived, led by Moira Lister. Lights powered on and the cyclorama changed to a distant horizon. Actors filled the lifeboat and others climbed into the tank and took position, holding onto the ropes draped at the lifeboat's sides. An order for silence rang out, echoing and re-echoing throughout the large studio. This was followed by the clapperboard routine and the final command for 'action'. The water in the tank started to move ominously, and gloom settled over the scene. The actors in the water lowered themselves so that only their heads appeared above water. Suddenly, everyone in and out of that lifeboat looked to be in dire peril. The water became really choppy and the unfortunates who were immersed spat out a mouthful every now and then. Stephen, who was not in shot, shouted out some

160

lines: 'Man the boats' – 'Women and children . . .' I thought I could feel a breeze coming off the sea, so realistic were the effects. It would all have been really convincing and I might well have been most concerned about people's safety, had it not been for the cameraman wearing waders standing in front of the lifeboat with camera in hand, rough water lapping his thighs.

When the scene was shot Stephen joined me and explained that he had to repeat his lines elsewhere as the sound men were not satisfied. We made our way to another studio, much smaller, where Stephen entered what looked like a telephone box. There was a glass viewing panel at one end of the studio, well lit and occupied by the director and the sound men, all wearing headphones. The whole business was accomplished in a matter of minutes, and Stephen and I retired to the canteen. Whilst we were tucking into roast beef and Yorkshire pudding, I noticed familiar faces at a table opposite; wearing striped blazers, open-necked shirts and white trousers were David Tomlinson, Laurence Harvey and Jimmy Edwards. At another table sat Charlie Chaplin in deep conference with a character who looked like an agent. Stephen informed me that Chaplin was making *A King in New York* and the others were in production of *Three Men in a Boat*. When we got to the coffee stage, I reminded my host that the last time we had had coffee together had been in Campbell's on the day of the Jewish joke, and that it had been my treat. His treat far outweighed mine, and I can still see his big dimpled grin, aware of the pleasure for which he was responsible.

During that unforgettable day, Stephen suggested that at some time he would like to commission a portrait. Naturally enough, I would have been delighted to paint him, but sadly, like many good intentions, we never got round to fulfilling the commission. Years later, after Stephen's sad demise, I was approached to do a drawing of him. This was for a copper memorial plaque which now hangs in the Queen's Film Theatre, and was unveiled by Sir Anthony Quayle.

Following a brilliant performance in Sam Thompson's *The Evangelist* in the Grand Opera House, Ray McAnally was feeling peckish, so Yvonne and myself sat down to a late meal with him in the Windsor café in Donegall Square South. Ray was certainly ravenous that night and, enthusiastic professional that he was, he was equally hungry to analyse his own performance. McAnally was good at everything connected with theatrical production, the possible exception being stage design (although I would not have bet against his abilities in that direction). He was an actor unashamedly proud of his abilities, to such an extent that he diminished his popularity with many fellow actors. However, there was no diminishing his power as a performer. When we left the Windsor it was around midnight, and Ray travelled back with us to Dundonald, where we lived when we were first married. Once home, we naturally talked theatre and Ray was in his element, giving us five different interpretations of the Evangelist character, each one a gem. When Ray left us that morning it was nearly 5 a.m., daylight was breaking and birdsong filled the air. We were very privileged to have had that superb demonstration of intimate theatre, a night and a memory to treasure. Despite his serious health problems, Ray remained a giant talent on the Irish theatre scene, and later started to make his presence felt in films. With his death the acting world suffered a major blow and theatre-lovers lost a unique talent. Those of us who knew him as a friend have lost a great deal more.

The late James Young, who became such a household name in his native land, used to say that he and I had much in common in our brand of humour. We could, he said, send up both sides of the religious divide without causing rancour. The most likely explanation for such a knack is that our humour was born of affection – the love for our people. We criticised constructively, pointing out the weaknesses and highlighting the strengths of the Irish. Never could either of us be accused of being destructively critical. His conviction that we had a parallel approach to humour prompted him to give me scripts, into which I would insert lines. Once, when there was a strike in the shipyard, I wrote a short four-minute sketch for him to perform on a BBC television news programme, in which he played four characters – a manager, a trade union man, a worker and his wife. I designed many of his programmes, and countless Christmas cards. A flamboyant character, Jimmy loved the star image. His house, Camelot, apart from its stagey name, had settings rather than rooms, where he luxuriated and expanded his considerable talents before those fortunate enough to be his guests. At such social events you could preview what might well be the embryonic forms of new sketches. The added talents of being an excellent host and a superb chef made all his at-homes gala performances.

James Young and his
straight man Jack Hudson

I remember guesting on a BBC television series he did many years back at the Balmoral studios, when he made reference to characters I drew, saying they were typical Ulster folk and could never be mistaken for anything else. This I disputed, simply because these so-called typically Ulster characters can be seen worldwide. I have observed what I considered to be a five o'clock shift from the shipyard board a train in Norway; at the Plaza de Toros in Spain I have seen those faces olé-ing; in Portugal, Italy, Denmark, wherever I have been, I have seen such types and they were not Irish tourists. Backdrops localise and authenticate the native. The twin cranes of Harland and Wolff, the Cave Hill, the city hall, backstreets, farmyards and stone dikes, all suggest the character's origin. Those men and women who inhabit the world of my cartoons are creations of the mind – a hotchpotch of faces and figures observed and lodged in the memory bank. Interesting noses, poses, ears, leers, strong chins, weak chins, no chins, hands, knees and bumps – they are all stored away. Unless they be actual caricatures – exaggerated likenesses – then they are simply composites of those features observed and remembered, reassembled and arranged to create a character from my mental identikit file. Any similarity to folk living or dead is a figment of the reader's wishful thinking. In addition to the setting, in many cases the wording of a caption contributes to pinpointing an area. Cartooning is the one form of pictorial art that scores heavily over all others for popularity. It is directly focused on life and the eye of the cartoonist is like a magnifier, recording and exposing all our faults and foibles. That 'man in the street' and all his friends enjoy and understand cartoons more readily than any other art form. With painting and sculpture becoming more and more obscure, and critics stimulating artists in the abstract, the poor wee man in the street and his friends are less inclined to rush to the galleries. Holding the abstract up to them is like presenting the cross to Dracula.

23

CAR-LESS RAPTURE

M Y EARLY VISITS TO THE TT races at Dundonald in the 1920s whetted my appetite for car racing, yet I have never driven a car. This fact few people can believe, in a world of mechanisation where a huge number of families have more than one car polluting air and pedestrian alike. Our three children, Vivien, Jeremy and Timothy all have cars, yet Yvonne and myself know naught of the auto. We believe clutches are grasps, gear is clothing and a big end an undesirable anatomical affliction. What makes this phenomenon seem all the more ludicrous is that I became a member of the Ulster Automobile Club and mixed enthusiastically with the racing fanatics. I even wore the club blazer with pride and strutted around as though I had just parked my MG Sports round the corner. My only explanation for this lack of what would seem to be one of life's necessities is that I never needed a car. At that age when motorcycles or cars become a youth's automatic fixation, I was consorting with my elders in the art world. When I went on sketching trips or had to travel to exhibitions, they rallied round with transport.

In addition to my colleagues in art, I had lots of friends in the car-racing fraternity. Ernie Robb, who had a garage at Dundonald and lived a few doors from me, had a friendly disposition and five specials, his wife Loubelle, daughter Norma, two sons David and Perry, and a racing car he built himself. It was through the Robbs that I became involved with the racing set and joined the automobile club. The friends I made among the speedsters added an exciting new dimension to my life. A greater fun crowd it would be very difficult to find. Their passion for cars was obsessive but never boring, and the competitive spirit was catching, even to a non-driver like myself. I went to trials with them, and races at the Curragh, Kirkiston and Dundrod. At one trial in the Newry area I actually navigated for Ernie Robb when he was driving his Mercury special. With narrow twisting roads and stone dikes hurtling towards me at the speed of foresight and the route map wrapping itself round my chest, it was not the easiest of tasks to keep a fully concentrating driver on course. The blur of passing trees and the scattering of panic-stricken chickens were inclined to distract an equally frightened navigator's mind from the task in hand. I cannot recall where Ernie finished on that occasion, but all credit to him that he managed to finish at all.

Another friend and car enthusiast, George Bryson, was to introduce me to an adventure in stark contrast to that of the Newry–Robb saga. George had just acquired one of the latest cars to take the motor show by storm – a Mini. Gripped by pride and excitement, George became impatient to 'run it in'. He decided to accomplish the running-in process by clocking up the requisite number of miles driving round the perimeter of Lough Neagh. Through some mental lapse, I accepted an invitation to join him in the exercise. We started off in boyish good humour, and enveloped as we were in the exciting smells of a brand-new car, all was, as Dr Pangloss philosophised, 'for the best, in the best of all possible worlds'. A leisurely – very leisurely – tour around the beautiful lough began and the conversation bubbled about the magic of the little car. We rolled along at about the speed of a prairie schooner, and when we had completed our eulogising on the wonders of his little gem we started to discuss our friends, their cars and their cares. Like the walrus and the carpenter, we talked of many things and we had not yet completed even one circuit of the lough. It is the biggest lake in the British Isles and I was beginning to be convinced that it must be the biggest in the world. We motored on, with Bryson's face locked in an expression of dogged determination, or perhaps hypnotic trance. Time passed even slower than the 'running-in' speed as the lough increased in size. As dusk was falling, I thought George waved a funeral cortège past, but I could have been hallucinating. How long it took us on that marathon, I know not, but we were both much older on its completion. Perhaps it was George and his Mini that created my lack of ambition towards car ownership.

My enthusiasm for the racing scene has never abated. Formula 1 Grand Prix, however, does not have the same thrill as the old road

racing. I was, on a couple of occasions, promoted to the position of Observer at the Dundrod Ulster Tourist Trophy. This involved the luxury of my own observation hut with earphones and direct communication with race control. It also made me commander in chief of my battle area and responsible for the marshals.

Those halcyon days of road racing had cars that looked like cars, all with their own personalities and not just a series of advertising projectiles. There were Frazer Nashes, Jaguars, MGs, BRMs, Allards and ERAs, all flashing past and all instantly identifiable. We had Mike Hawthorn and Stirling Moss, locals Bobby Baird and Desmond Titterington, plus the mystery of the east in the form of the White Mouse Stables, Prince Bira and Prince Chula, with their blue-clad retinue and yellow and blue ERAs bearing the White Mouse symbol, all adding extra glamour to the scene. Drivers from north, south, east and west all converged on the County Antrim circuit to put their expertise to the test and, to some extent, revive the famous Ulster Tourist Trophy Race.

Sadly, Dundrod was never to attain the worldwide reputation of the Ards circuit, which had ended so tragically with a horrific crash in Newtownards in September 1936, when local man Jack Chambers lost control and crashed into a crowd of spectators, killing eight people.

24

SOUND AND VISION

" Calm yourselves. The news to-night is terrible."

I REMEMBER MY BROTHER BILL making a wireless set. I was fascinated by all the tiny bits and pieces he laid out on the table before him. The smell of soldering, the concentration he displayed, and the final satisfaction on his face at the completion of his crystal set, all helped me to realise the importance of this very new medium of communication. I can recall the weird screechings, noises like sea breaking on foreign shores, now and then a disjointed and distant sound of some conversation, a distorted note of music. Then suddenly, we had clear reception and proper sound. Bill had succeeded. He had caught up with Marconi and 2LO was with us. Little did I dream that, with the passing of the years, I should be adding my own voice. From those times of the disembodied, even ethereal, voices to the present startling realism of stereophonic sound, we have come a long, long way.

The cartooning side of my art has been the key that has opened many doors. When you are by profession a commentator on human behaviour, and shoot the sartirical darts, you are in demand. Invitations poured in for talks, panels and chat shows. The radio, with its insatiable appetite, was perpetually on the prowl for people and material. I can bring to mind one very early broadcast on *The Arts in Ulster*, when a problem arose, a problem which surfaces constantly to this very day. Ian and I were settled in the talks studio with the interviewer, Nelson Browne, who at that time had left teaching to join the BBC. The series was produced by John Boyd, and he had discussed exactly the way he would like the programme to go. We were sitting chatting with one eye on the red light bulb when the studio door opened and the announcer entered and hurriedly whispered in my ear.

'I've always wondered about the correct pronunciation of your

167

name,' he said. 'Is it "Roal Freers" or "Raoul Friers"?'

'The latter is correct,' I informed him.

He thanked me profusely, saying he was glad to get it right and hastily retreated to the announcer's booth. The red light glowed, and through our earphones we heard the announcement: 'Tonight, in *The Arts in Ulster*, we have the two artist brothers, Ian and Roal Freers.'

One time I rang my friend Leslie Stuart, the photographer, who had a new receptionist to whom I was a complete stranger.

'May I speak to Mr Stuart, please?' I asked.

'Sorry, he's not in' came the reply.

'Oh well, tell him Rowel Friers rang.'

'Who?'

Thinking my diction was possibly a bit ropey, I enunciated: 'ROWEL FRIERS.'

My friend the photographer Leslie Stuart and myself (Courtesy of Leslie Stuart)

'Sorry, I don't get it,' she said.

Another try at 'Rowel Friers' brought no more joy. She still hadn't got it. 'Oh, just tell him his artist friend rang.' I tried not to growl.

'Ah,' she gasped in ecstasy, 'Rolf Harris!'

I retired huffily to my drawing board and tried to draw Bugs Bunny à la Harris. What's in a name? A lot, say I.

With a moniker like mine, you are well-nigh exclusive. When Bill was working on a Canadian battleship during the war he met two lieutenants who were close pals, one called Rowel and the other Friers – a remarkable coincidence.

The Stuart phone call was upstaged, I feel, by an incident outside Ulster Television in the 1960s. I was coming out of Havelock House in the early days of the station when kids hung around looking for autographs. Anyone who came out of that building was often erroneously presumed to be a celebrity of some kind, and they hovered like vultures. A scruffy kid with an equally scruffy jotter ran up to me and asked 'Mister' for his autograph. At the time I was drawing a series by Shelia St Clair entitled *Danny the Dormouse*, so in the jotter I wrote 'Danny the Dormouse' and underneath it scrawled my name. The youngster took his book, the eyes lit up with delight, and in a very loud shriek, summoned a temporarily invisible crony.

'Hi, Jimmy, stickin' out! I've got Danny the Dormouse.' This, followed by a pause, and a baffled expression, as he studied the jotter. He looked up at me, pointed a none-too-clean finger at my signature, and asked, 'Mister, who the hell's that?'

Once I was giving a talk to Campbell College art club, to which I had been invited by their art teacher, the late Helen Anderson. The room was packed with pupils, all on their best behaviour and extremely attentive. The easel had a large sketching pad on it and, as is my wont, I sketched as I talked – a sure way of holding attention. When the talk was completed I threw the meeting open to questions. There was the usual flow of obvious enquiries, but one suddenly came out of the blue. In actual fact it came from a window at the back of the room, on the sill of which a couple of boys sat.

'Sir' – with hand raised – 'what does it feel like to be famous?'

It was a stinker! I had to think of what sort of pose to strike, and what expression to adopt, all in the short time it took for the question to register.

'I must think about that for a second,' I countered. Then it came to me and I gave my answer, thus: 'In Ireland we had only one humorous magazine, called *Dublin Opinion*. *Dublin Opinion* had CEK or, you might say, CEK had *Dublin Opinion*, because he was one of its owners. He also was a director of Radio Éireann, and a cartoonist who drew jokes, mainly dealing with the civil service and governmental gyrations. His appeal was, therefore, limited. Then there was William Conn, one of the best pen-and-ink artists in Ireland, but he didn't do humorous cartoons. His drawings were mainly of Georgian tenements with ghostly figures, from a gracious past, full of sentiment and nostalgia. Also we had Billy Glenn, who did scraperboard work for *Dublin Opinion* and this, though whimsical, was not funny, and fell more into the category of illustration.

'None of those aforementioned could be classed as being in the same vein as myself. However, we did have two brilliantly funny men, Maskee (Bill Beckett) and NO'K (Neil O'Kennedy). Maskee, sadly died, and Neil O'Kennedy packed it in and went to advertising. This, then, left me as the only full-time professional cartoonist in existence in Ireland at that time. To answer the original question: it is rather like being heavyweight boxing champion of the Copeland Islands.'

25

ANOTHER MEDIUM

PRESSURE IS THE NAME OF THE GAME where cartooning is concerned. Newspapers and magazines have deadlines and if those deadlines are not met, you may join the breadline. Early in my career when I was working for magazines, I learned that to succeed you need to be dependable, and this meant having your contribution in before the deadline. It was not easy in the beginning, particularly during *Dublin Opinion* days, when I had to turn out eight to ten different jokes per issue. None of the cartoons was topical, my work then being general in theme. Those were the days when you sat with a blank board before you, and a matching mind, a time when you had the whole world to draw on – targets galore, a glut of subject matter, like a huge box of chocolates laid before you, and you could not decide which one to choose. As the years pass, and observation and knowledge of your fellow man improves, this problem of selection diminishes rapidly. Your maturing attitude towards life is reflected in the images you create.

Topical cartoons are much easier than the non-topical because a weak crack can be carried by its sheer topicality. Once I had mastered the pressure of the magazine and newspaper worlds, my confidence was at its highest. This peak, however, was but a foothill in comparison with what was to follow.

My introduction, in the late 1950s, to the hustle and bustle of television and its voracious appetite started with an invitation from dear old Auntie Beeb to take a weekend crash course in preparation for the introduction of local programming. It was a really enlightening experience for me being in a class where the instructors were as vague as the students. We were shown how to, and how not to, interview people, how to do a commentary without blemish, and all of it live. Films of

Richard Dimbleby running on and off the rails, Raymond Baxter interviewing in the right and wrong ways, were shown as part of the educational programme. We rehearsed from ten in the morning until nine in the evening and had a final run-through from nine until half-nine. The first transmission was *Preview 1* (broadcast closed circuit as *Studio 8*) on Friday 16 January 1959, producer Robert Coulter, going out in the evening from ten until ten-thirty.

The coolest man in the studios, or he who gave the greatest impression as such, was that super-professional Michael Baguley. Taking part in this very first programme were Michael Baguley, Sam Napier, Eric Waugh, Martin Wallace, Tom Roberts, David Hammond, Francis McPeake, and myself – the first faces to be transmitted on local television.

With the arrival of television, the pressure of the press was reduced to a dawdle. Programmes I became involved in like *The Irish RM* and the stories of Lynn Doyle on Ulster Television, with the late Charlie Witherspoon as storyteller, required as many as forty drawings to cover the viewing time. Payment for such work was minimal, making it imperative that you did not take more than a day and a half to complete the lot. Once in possession of the script it was my task to break it up into visuals. I would mark out those passages which lent themselves to illustration, and, once convinced that the chosen visuals dramatised the story sufficiently, I would go to work. Because television was in black and white in those days, silver-grey boards were used to avoid glare. At first I used the normal method of black and white drawing, that is, Indian ink and drawing pen, white paint for highlights and black crayon for texture and shading. I was soon to learn that the ordinary pen that required constant dipping into the ink bottle was much too slow. To speed matters up I started to use felt pens. By eliminating the constant dipping and by introducing the rapid, indeed instant, drying felt pen I cut my time to one-third of that taken on the first few programmes.

The secret of illustrating such programmes with forty or more drawings was to use the 'hidden persuader' technique – hoodwinking the viewer. Of the forty drawings, about eight would be very detailed and the rest would be fast impressions. For instance, if you were doing a hunting scene, then a three- or four-foot drawing would be created, showing horses tumbling, jumping or refusing. The riders would all be the recognisable characters you had created from the story and each

expression would reflect their thoughts about taking the jump. The detail in that particular visual would mean that the camera could pan slowly along the drawing, stop here and there, and even zoom in on close-ups, the draughtsmanship being such that it could stand examination. The remainder of the drawings in the set would be much more sketchy and loosely drawn, but they would have to suggest action and facial expressions. These ones would appear as a mere flash on the screen, but the more careful drawings, having already registered style and mood in the viewer's mind, would, and did, complete the deception that the images were all of an equal standard.

I only discovered this speedy approach after a few marathons. The BBC series of Percy French songs – 'Slattery's Mountain Foot', 'Phil the Fluter's Ball', 'Are Ye Right There Michael?' and so on – were all most detailed and done with the time-consuming dipping method. As Brendan O'Dowda sang, the illustrations would embellish the story. Milo O'Shea recited some of the French poems, but these were not illustrated. Brendan now has a four-foot drawing of 'Phil the Fluter's Ball' hanging in his home.

It was one of those twenty-four-hour flu-type bugs. My bug produced a combination of a head like the engine room of the old Heysham ferry,

Doc, I think I have a bad touch of the 'Flu!

two aching eyeballs, a Niagara nose, muscles I never knew I had and whose function seemed to be merely to throb, plus a back that housed a built-in cold-running shower. Frankly, I was not at my best. The phone rang like a fire engine's bell, and as fast as my aching limbs could move, I lifted the receiver. A sickeningly jolly voice, full of excess energy, played a tattoo on my eardrums. Tony Finnegan wanted me at Havelock House (Ulster Television's HQ) immediately, to do three illustrations for a programme scheduled for transmission at 6.30 p.m. that day. The phone attack was timed at 11.30 a.m. 'No' would not be accepted as an answer; they would send an ambulance, if necessary. The phone had barely reached its cradle when a noisy taxi arrived at my front door, and after a journey over what seemed to be a very rough country lane, I was grounded at Havelock House. Tony was delighted to see me, and taking my complaints as modest protests of my unworthiness for such an important project, he ushered me into the design room and vanished. Resident designer Roy Gaston indicated where script and board awaited me and having observed my obviously deteriorating state of health, drew himself in, tortoise-like, and markedly increased his

174

concentration on his own design. Intuitively, I felt that after that one look at me, Gaston was panicking with the thought that he was now trapped in an isolation ward.

I focused the aching eyeballs on the script, which was a story about country folk. The little concentration that I still possessed prompted me to start drawing. I laboured through two illustrations with electric currents running up my back, adding power to the thundering head. Every now and then a hot drip from my nose would splash on the back of my hand as an added complication to a tortuous ordeal. It was 3.00 p.m. or thereabouts before I finished those two visuals. I had not eaten and had no desire to do so, but my head was killing me, and I was so caught up in the ague that my teeth had adopted a flamenco rhythm. Help was needed. I could not go on. I made a dash for Tony's office and crashed in on him after virtually knocking the door off its hinges.

'Tony, I need something to help this condition. I feel rigor mortis is about to set in. I'm freezing.'

It is very irritating when somebody is so damned healthy that they can smilingly assure you everything will be all right. Such was Tony on that fateful day. He walked calmly to his cupboard, took out a bottle of Bush, and poured what looked to me like half the bottle.

'Drink that. It'll take away the shivers,' he said.

I drank it slowly, all of it, and it knocked me back. My heating system went to boiling point and with what I imagined was a cool wave of thanks, I opened one of the two doors and left to tackle the third and most difficult drawing.

Empty stomachs and full glasses are not the best prescription for competence, and here I was facing the toughest task of all – a jaunting car with a full load cavorting along a country road. The jaunting car is far from easy to draw, particularly from memory, and much more difficult to draw when that memory is complicated by trying to work out how you have made your way back to the studio. A strange, cavalier attitude had taken over and 'who gives a damn anyway' was my thinking as I threw myself into that final drawing. It was completed in half, or even a quarter, of the time it took me to do the other pair. A taxi was ordered, and I returned home luxuriating on the same road, which now appeared to have kerb-to-kerb carpeting.

My instincts told me I must watch that programme, and I had the strongest misgivings that number three would be avant-avant-garde. I fell into a deep sleep in front of the televison set. The theme tune of the programme wakened me and I waited with bated Bush-laden breath to see how that last drawing had turned out. When they appeared on the screen, the first two showed the struggle and agony, but in the last, the jaunting car was fairly flying, the horse and passengers were all full of life and jollity, super action and utter ecstasy. The drawing lived, and I fell into a contented sleep.

When Ulster Television first ventured forth with their outside broadcast unit and *Gloria Plus* (hosted by Gloria Hunniford), they chose Bangor as their location. The leisure centre was packed and buzzing with excitement and the television crew were even more excited as they tried to cope with their first essay into outdoor broadcasting. Amongst those to appear in the programme were the singer Johnny Logan, comedian Adrian Walsh, my old pal, actor Jimmy Ellis, and myself. The make-up people went to work on us and the pancake was applied, reducing our faces to creamy-coloured death masks. It is remarkable how the generous application of make-up eradicates all facial expression and leaves you looking like a window-dresser's model. As time ticked slowly away, the audience excitement had noticeably reduced in volume as boredom set in. Amongst the technicians, panic was admirably controlled and the swearing was barely audible as they wrestled with a complexity of snaking cables and a plethora of plugs. Time raced for the workers and dragged for the watchers.

Ellis, whose patience I would classify as suspect, particularly in a hang-around situation, came over to me and growled, 'Let's go for a bloody drink. They'll be a while sortin' this out.'

'Do you think we should?' I asked nervously. 'They might get it all together as soon as we leave the centre.'

I am one of those characters who, if he is asked to sit and wait in a certain spot, will do so, and remain there like an obedient dog until called. To get out of sight, to me, is definitely to get out of mind, so I was somewhat reluctant to accept my friend's suggestion.

'Come on. We'll only be a couple of minutes, and these bloody lights have me dehydrated,' reasoned Jimmy.

The professionalism of Ellis is most convincing. A sudden change of set found us in shot in a bar in Bangor's Main Street. Jimmy's pint of beer looked like a bucket and my whiskey and ginger looked like a pint. AWOL does that to me. As we stood there chatting, a very affable

176

character came over and joined us. Oh, my God, I thought, we are in for a session and more 'outdoor' than *Gloria Plus* had intended.

'You're Sergeant Lynch, aren't you?' said the affable one.

'No, he was Inspector Lynch when that programme ended,' I answered hastily, as Jimmy's nose was in his bucket of beer. Haste we needed, and not a catalogue of Jimmy's achievements.

Affability looked me up and down with a strange expression in his eyes. 'I do a bit of art work myself,' he said, searching my face for conclusive evidence that I was who he thought I was. His expression had, I thought, lost a little of its chumminess and turned a trifle contemptuous. But, worse than that, he seemed determined to create an interview situation which, without doubt, would outlast Gloria Hunniford's.

'Well, Big Man, how's about you?' he said, dismissing me with obvious disdain and turning to Jimmy, who had just resurfaced from the bucket. 'You were in *Z Cars*. I remember you well,' he continued.

'I was indeed,' answered the Big Man, once more plunging into his bucket. Panic was getting to me, and I muttered something about the time. Over the edge of his bucket Jimmy gave me a knowing glance. Message received. I gulped down my whiskey and ginger, and Jimmy placed his empty vessel on the counter.

'Fancy another?' asked the stranger – pointedly ignoring me.

Jimmy looked at him for the first time, having freed himself of his drink. 'No, thank you, we're in a hurry,' said Ellis. 'It's most kind of you but we have to go.'

The stranger looked hard at Jimmy as he had at me, and his expression visibly soured. 'Ach well, if you have to go, you have to go,' he muttered, and sidled off hurriedly.

We made for the door and back to the leisure centre. The man's face kept coming into my mind – his affability and that remarkable change in expression to uncertainty, disbelief, and then ill-concealed contempt. I wondered about that.

'Funny bugger, that,' said Jimmy.

'He was,' I answered.

Then I smelled it, a delicate perfume – the pancake make-up.

'You know why he was funny, Jimmy?' I queried.

'Why do you think?' he asked.

'He thought we were an odd couple – damn it, we're both wearing make-up!'

James Ellis (Courtesy of Jeremy Friers)

Just as Wilfred Pickles was the first BBC newsreader to introduce dialect to the listening public, so, I believe, Jimmy Ellis, with his long run in *Z Cars*, acclimatised British ears to the nuances and subtleties of the Northern Ireland dialect. It was he who opened doors to the talents of the North, of that I am convinced. All those actors, comics and presenters who have since invaded the British studios (and become known as the Murphia) owe that rugged east-ender a great debt of gratitude.

There was also the late and great Colin Blakely, a friend of mine from his amateur days, who added considerably to the rise of the Northern Irish accent. Apparently, it was thanks to his friendship with Colin that Robert Shaw learned to perfect his accent for his role in *The Sting*. Who will forget his much used phrase: 'Do ya falla?'

178

26

LEFT ALONE AND MELANCHOLIA

IT WAS 1964 AND I WAS IN hospital with an ulcer recurrence when
Cambridge came and told me that Mother had died. Crushing news.
That was an afternoon visit which left me with plenty of time to
reason and console myself before the approach of dusk. Mother had
lived a good, long, constructive life, and to reach the age of eighty-six
was, after all, no minor innings. The crisis periods of her long life she
faced with determination and had proven herself to be a fearless lady.

Such were the comforting thoughts I fed myself in that hospital bed,
preparatory to meeting the night I feared. Hospitals at night are not, at
any time, conducive to peaceful sleep, particularly if you are at all sen-
sitive to surroundings. Darkness followed dusk, and the night staff the
day; the ward lights dimmed with my spirits. The earlier preparations
and philosophisings were to prove a complete waste of time. However
much I tried to dismiss Mother's death from my mind, the more
hopeless it got. She would be buried and I could not attend her funeral.
That thought tortured me. Gradually the ward settled down for the
night and the long rows of beds on either side took on a blue, ghostly
appearance. My own bed light blazed brightly and my tortured mind
went into overdrive. I tossed and turned within the limited scope permitted by the stricture of a saline drip. The nurse arrived at my bedside
on her lights-out round.

'What's wrong, Mr Friers? Can't you sleep?'

I told her what was wrong, and the reason for my sleeplessness.

'I'll get you something to help you sleep,' she volunteered.

I was greatly relieved, and thanked her. I watched her walk off down
the blue length of that ward. Although she returned in a couple of
minutes, it seemed a tense hour. She gave me sleeping tablets and

assured me they would relax me. An hour later, seeing my light still burning, she came back to find me still wide awake and more tense than ever. I could not sleep, it was hopeless, and I told her so.

'You must relax,' she told me, 'it is bad for you not to get some rest. How can I help you?' was her kind enquiry. 'What would you usually do to relax?'

'I suppose I would draw,' I answered.

'Right, I'll go and find you some materials,' she said, rising and gliding swiftly and silently down the ward.

Another period of tortured time elapsed before she returned smiling, carrying a sketch pad and pencil. I do not know where she managed to get those materials at that hour, but get them she did. Not only did she get me the means to redirect my thoughts, but she sat with me until the pencil fell from my grasp and sleep intervened. Nurses like that should be paid as much as, if not more than, a lot of doctors. Real feeling for patients goes a long long way in defeating many maladies.

Bill, or William Richard, became head of the family when Father died in 1926, or at least male head because Mother was always head, even when Father was alive. It was Bill, more than anyone else, who encouraged me to read the classics, starting with *Swiss Family Robinson*, through *Treasure Island*, all of Henty, Rider Haggard, Jeffrey Farnol, to *Lorna Doone*, *Wuthering Heights*, and Dickens. Ian got me interested in Smollett and Voltaire and together they made sure I did not hang on to the *Wizard* or the *Rover* for too long. Bill's hobby was mathematics. He loved the subject and could never understand why I was such a dumb-bell at school. He was twenty years older than me, and Cambridge and himself could have been my father and mother. What an advantage I had, and how lucky I was to have had a family older and wiser than myself, who took a real interest in me as a youngster. After Father's death Bill had to take a job; he became an engineer and worked in Harland and Wolff's. He spent a period working in England, tool-making with de Havilland, and a period on an oil tanker plying back and forth to Aruba. Bill was quiet and studious, with no patience for stupidity or ignorance, and as well as being practical he was, I feel, the most academic of us all. His handwriting, too, was remarkable, a flowing copperplate. It was he who paid me the greatest compliment I ever had. We were in a bar in Holywood, and over a drink I asked him why he had never kept up his drawing.

'Rowel,' he said, 'when I saw how well you could draw at the age of twelve, I gave up.'

Bill never married. He must have been the father figure too long, or took to heart Mother's dire warning: 'Watch the wimmin. They're only looking for a soft seat!'

His life was ended by a hit-and-run driver in November 1975. Bill always said he wanted to go quickly and that was how it was. Ian, who had been ill for quite a period and was in hospital at that time, died three days later, leaving his wife Rene, three sons, Roderick, Julian and Quentin, and two daughters, Cindy and Zoe.

To lose two brothers inside three days is a devastating experience, with which few could really cope. With that hideously cruel experience I seemed to go icy cold, feelingless, almost robotic. Here I was, faced with two funerals, things I knew nothing about, and a situation I would never have imagined I could manage. That strange change in my personality, the coldness that enveloped me, had the remarkable effect of

transforming me into a super-efficient organiser. Every melancholy detail relating to funeral arrangements was carried out with a cool efficiency that I would have thought to be beyond my capabilities. Utterly emotionless, barely polite to relatives and friends, everyone must have been convinced that I was completely heartless. To a certain extent, they would have been right. I was not only heartless, I was completely withdrawn and I am convinced the topic among a lot of those attending the funeral was my apparent insensitivity.

A few days after the cremations, when my son and I carried two small caskets containing the ashes to the memorial garden by St Elizabeth's Church in Dundonald, I must surely have shocked the canon. I looked at the two neat little boxes and could not withhold the odd remark, 'Well, there go my two wee brothers.' Whether the canon actually heard me, I know not, but I received no look of disapproval. However, I am positive that both Bill and Ian would have appreciated the black comedy. Indeed, for all I know, they may well have laughed together somewhere out there on that melancholy day.

After the trauma of that double bereavement, it happened. The real me surfaced once more. I went to the phone, placed my finger in the digital hole, and started to dial Dundonald 2136. My finger stopped in mid-air halfway through the dialling when the horrible realisation gripped me. They were dead. No more could I ring them for a chat. The close bonds that had held us had been broken, I was now alone. 'Gone for ever' was hard to take. It was impossible to imagine a world without my two brothers, brothers who had encouraged me in every possible way to reach towards that goal I had set myself. It was a cruel loss, the horrible truth of which only struck me three weeks later.

That tough façade I had had when organising the funerals fell apart and I developed agonising intestinal pains. With the pains I drifted into deep melancholia. My doctor could do little to help me, though he did try hard. The pains would not ease, and the melancholia grew deeper; sleep was fitful and any that came held dreams of nightmarish form; rest was impossible. I withdrew into the shell that was my body, and thought of nothing except the pains that gripped my interior. My doctor sent me to a specialist, the same one who had looked after Ian. He told me that my own GP thought I was suffering from tension, and after a thorough examination, he also believed this to be the case. I was sceptical and told him that I considered the pains to be a lot more than tension. He said my trouble was that I had the same pains Ian had suffered, but not the same ailment. Psychosomatic sympathetic symptoms were diagnosed, and to eliminate any doubts I had – and there were plenty – he said he would give me a bowel barium. That hellishly embarrassing and very uncomfortable operation was performed and I was given the all-clear. Such an assurance would comfort most, but it did not really do much for me, I just stayed inside my tortured mind and sat around the house. What a strain it must have been for Yvonne and our family, a considera-tion to which such patients as I never give a thought.

To shave was to look in a mirror, and that was something I could not bear to do. The face that looked back at me was not mine: grey and drawn, with eyes that stared through me, haunted and alien. I had to avoid that terrifying confrontation. When I shaved I just turned my head to one side, only reflecting the chin, and this enabled me to avoid the tortured stranger. It was quite a few months before I pulled out of that loss of health induced by the loss of my brothers. I was not, after all, the heart of stone some may have thought me to be.

Big sister, as I called Cambridge, was, as the Americans would put it, really something else. Like my mother, she was strong-willed, witty, bright and, when occasion called, she could cut you down like a scythe. Like Mother and Bill, she was a redhead. Fashion-conscious, as behoves the mannequin she became, she was supremely confident, well-read, and strikingly attractive. In the era of the flapper, she could charleston and blackbottom with the best. She referred to me as Baby until I was about fifteen, and I was used as an excuse for boys she did not like or trust – she 'had to look after Baby'. She married Fraser Mayne and, by doing so, ensured I would have a constant supply of art materials. Fraser encouraged me tremendously with a never-ending stream of top-quality products from the firm's stationery department. Cambridge Elizabeth, called variously Camie, Camilla or Cammy, had much the same name trouble as myself. She and Fraser had a family of two, a son Terence and a daughter Stephanie. When the children were still young, Fraser began seeing another woman, and on hearing of this, my sister took up a poker and Fraser took to his heels! A divorce was the natural outcome. I missed Fraser and, fortunately for him, so did the poker.

Cambridge looked after an invalid friend, Helen Moore, until her death, and after a period married Helen's husband Billy. Both Fraser and Billy predeceased her and she died in July 1991 aged eighty-seven, mentally alert and witty to the end. She claimed to be an atheist and as she lay dying instructed me to have no clergy at her funeral service.

'I want you to have "The Lark in the Clear Air" played,' she told me, 'and I want you to think of the lark as me, flying high and free.'

'The Continental' was played at her funeral, appropriate background music for a girl of the twenties and thirties. 'The Lark' was played too, and although she did not want flowers I thought a single rose was a must. Dr Mervum Gifford, her young neighbour, spoke an affectionate tribute, and Terence talked of the happy childhood she had created for his sister and himself and quoted some of her favourite lines: 'I am the master of my fate, I am the captain of my soul.'

Cambridge spent the last days of her life in the hospice on the Somerton Road. On 29 June 1991 Queen Elizabeth paid a state visit to Northern Ireland and took in the hospice as part of her programme. She visited my sister's bedside but Cambridge was now unaware. Her Majesty had a few words with her daughter Stephanie before moving on. Shortly afterwards, Cambridge died peacefully in her sleep.

27

BACK TO SCHOOL

ENPRASE, WHO HAD SO EXPERTLY guided me through my art
school days, was strongly opposed to my taking a teaching post
when I had finished my studies. He thought, rightly as it turned
out, that such an occupation would never suit me and could in fact be
disastrous. The indisposition of a friend, Eddie Johnston, was to prove
Penprase's point. In 1970 Eddie, who was a senior art master in Park
Parade school, had to be hospitalised for a couple of weeks to undergo
a throat operation, and someone was needed to fill in for him. The then
headmaster of the school, Sam Cuddy, approached me.

'How would you like to have a shot at teaching?' he asked.

'You must be joking,' I replied, although I knew full well that the
same man was not given to such jesting. I considered the pros and cons
for a minute or two – long enough for a foolish ego to take over. 'Why
not?' I decided. 'It should be an experience.'

How right I was.

The life of a teacher – short hours, long holidays, and getting paid for
it – was not what I had imagined. Once I had been thrown in at the
deep end, my imaginings were drastically and very rapidly dispelled. The
first sadly inaccurate notion was that I would be teaching a class of
youngsters who had an interest in art. Never in my wildest dreams did
I think I would be coping with streams of potential Philistines of varying
ages, whose faces and sexes changed to the sound of a deafening bell.

It was very early in the first week that I realised why teachers had long
holidays, and I wondered how many weeks of those holidays they spent
in rest homes. When you went to the staff room at break and witnessed
strong men staggering in, muttering veiled threats towards certain
pupils, kicking furniture or aiming karate blows at a table, a different

picture was painted. When women teachers whispered meaningfully amongst themselves and their teacups rattled in their hands like castanets, it struck me that this was clearly not a sinecure.

On my first morning I was greeted by a question from a keen youngster who asked, 'What do you think of Dr Paisley?'

I gave the appearance of being stumped and made the enquiry, 'Where does he practise and is he a good doctor?'

The boy looked baffled and stared around at the rest of his classmates, all of whom looked blank.

'Does he have a big surgery?' I asked, attempting to further my own education.

'He's not that kinda dacter,' the lad retorted, with all the contempt he could muster.

'Oh, he's not, I see . . . what is he then?'

'He's a manaster and a palatician.'

The whole class nodded their heads in confirmation and with a communal expression of incredulity.

'Sorry, son, I never heard of him,' I lied, with what I imagined was a beatific expression.

There was an audible gasp of disbelief from the assembled fan club. Without doubt I had created an impression.

This introductory approach to teaching was to be the way I would carry on. They would naturally assume, and correctly so, that I was a political innocent. They would also have already learned, gossip travelling as fast as it does, that I had attended Park Parade and must therefore be a Prod, and so be granted their seal of approval.

A boy in one of the classes had a different question to be answered. He wished to know – 'What's wrong with oul' Janti?'

'Who is oul' Janti?' I enquired.

'Wur teacher, sur' came the cultured retort.

'Oh, you mean Mr Johnston?'

'Aye.'

'Well, he has gone to hospital with a genetic ailment,' I lied.

'Wha's that?'

'Those of you who can read newspapers, or even watch the news on television, may have read or heard a few months ago about President Johnston of the USA.'

A couple of the brighter ones had heard, or pretended they had, that

186

President Johnston had had a throat operation.

'That throat condition,' I went on to explain, 'is a Johnston family weakness, and your Mr Johnston, who, incidentally, is a nephew of the president, has not escaped the curse of his tribe.'

The class was suitably impressed, one gathered, from a noise which closely resembled that of a tyre going down. I never learned whether or not they stopped calling Eddie 'Oul' Janti' after being enlightened about his illustrious lineage.

The senior boys, or junior Mafia class, I found tricky enough. Some of these boys would have made Attila the Hun feel nervous, and to attempt to teach them art would have been as sensible as taking them for ballet lessons. Those of them who were not already shaving, should have been. I could spot a clique who stuck close together, and also detect, without being a Poirot, that they had a leader. I knew I would have to watch this character above all others. I talked to them about cartoons, how they were created and printed. It held their interest, particularly when I did the drawings on the blackboard and they just had to loll back and listen. The arrangement suited us both.

One morning it happened. I felt it had to come sooner or later, but this was sooner than anticipated. Walking past the desk of the Godfather, I was stopped by a large hand taking hold of my coat tail.

'Nice bit of suit you have there, sir.'

He put a lot of emphasis on the 'sir', which elicited the desired attention from his leering cohorts. This, I realised, was not a healthy situation. He was much bigger than me – the hired gun and the town softie. A man's got to do what a man's got to do, and I nearly did it right then. However, I mastered my feelings of panic and, using my Thespian training, assumed a very deadpan expression.

'Yes, isn't it a nice bit of suiting?' I said, in what, at the time, I imagined was a chilling tone. 'And what a nice bit of suiting you have. Make it yourself?'

He was at a loss. I had taken a bold step that was obviously unexpected. His pals looked on, awaiting developments.

'Boy,' I said, releasing his hand with polite, almost delicate, care, and taking his two lapels in my hands, 'you have a natural sense of the ridiculous. I can see a future for you on television.'

The cronies were now smiling and, I hoped, were on my side.

'You would be a big hit on *Romper Room*.'

The canned laughter was turned on and I had won the day. He and his pals were quite matey with me after that incident.

Another difficult confrontation occurred in that class, when a large boy built like a Sumo wrestler rose and made his way to the door.

'Where do you think you are going, boy?' I demanded.

'Ah'm goin' to the lavitry,' said he.

'Oh, no, you're not. You are going back to that desk and you are going to raise your hand and ask my permission to leave the room.'

He looked at me in amazement.

'Please return to your desk at once and do as I have asked, or wet your trousers.'

He shuffled back, much to the amusement of the class. I told him that was the way I was trained in school and I saw no reason why he should not do likewise.

My greatest challenge was from the senior girls, with their traces of pink lipstick, eyes touched up, earrings and, in lots of instances, a walk that would have competed with Marilyn Monroe. My first morning with them I was greeted with, 'Mornin', handsome', all in chorus as they entered. On one occasion I found it necessary to bend down and pick up some paper nonchalantly dropped to the floor, like the lace hanky ploy used for another form of pick-up. As I regained the perpendicular the lassie responsible said in a loud voice, 'Girls, teacher's feelin' my leg.' Teacher managed a sickly smile; the class managed much more.

On another occasion I got fed up looking at the pathetic efforts of one rather languid female.

'Observe,' I said, 'and think what you are doing. The head is like an egg. There's roughly seven heads to the body.'

I started sketching for her and talking. All the other girls, without a by your leave, drifted over like brides of Dracula and stood around watching me draw. When I thought I had done enough sketching and lecturing I handed her back the pencil.

'Sure, if I take that home, my ma will niver believe that I did it,' she said.

'Ach, just tell her you had a genius in class who taught you overnight,' I suggested.

She tucked her chin into one shoulder, looked around from under long blond tresses, stuck her elbow in my ribs, and in a Lauren Bacall voice said, 'I wish it was overnight, sir.'

A titter arose from the brides of Dracula as they returned to their resting places.

Teaching, like preaching, must be one of the toughest of all professions, where you need all the patience of Job, the wisdom of Solomon, the attitude of the Samaritan, and 'look not to lay up treasure upon earth'. After the first week, teaching bored the hell out of me. The then Minister for Education, Bill Long, asked me how I enjoyed my stint. I told him I could never have taught those kids art. My conviction was that they were in that class to escape something else – they probably looked on it as a rest period. I would have preferred to play football with them – and I mean with them, not a ball. Penprase was so right.

Attending a retirement dinner in honour of the *Belfast Telegraph*'s sports editor, Malcolm Brodie, I made a short speech before the presentation. When I was a pupil at Park Parade it was not at all like the penitentiary it had become. We did not loll in our seats, we had respect for our teachers, plus a little fear here and there, and some we actually loved. The school proudly claimed four distinguished ex-pupils who had made the headlines. One was Malcolm Brodie, and the others were the singer Ronnie Carroll, the Bishop of Down and Dromore, Gordon McMullan, and myself. In the speech I said that among those four there was only one genius.

The journalists roared with one accord, 'That was yourself.'

'No,' I replied.

'It wasn't Brodie?' they enquired.

'No, it was Gordon McMullan. Anyone who could leave Park Parade and become a bishop *must* have been a genius.'

28

GRAPHIC DESCRIPTIONS

ONE OF MY PET AVERSIONS AS AN ARTIST has always been the kind of person who commissions you because he likes the way you think, and your style of drawing – the type who is very sure he makes right decisions. He is looking for a new approach to his market presentation, and he knows you are what he wants. His is a firm that has been in existence for one hundred years plus, and he is grandson of the founder. They produce, let us say, linen in all forms – pillowcases, counterpanes, bed linens of every sort, tablecloths, napkins. In his wood-panelled spacious office, behind a leather-topped desk that bears the ring marks of glasses dating back to grandfather, he sits. In a loud, authoritative voice he thanks you for coming, and hopes you will be able to help him out with his little problem. It is actually a big problem, but if it is described as little, it is a ploy to keep down the price.

'Care for a whiskey? sherry? coffee?', he will ask, fairly projecting friendliness. You opt for coffee to ensure your concentration will be unimpaired. This pleases him, because the coffee choice makes less impression on the firm's debit columns. He is the sort of person who, though he may give an Oscar-winning performance as a prosperous, affable and friendly being, is a Scrooge at heart. Usually the coffee is carried in by a little old lady of indeterminate age, who probably joined the firm at the same time as the desk.

'Will that be all? Will there be anything else?' she will quaver.

'That will be fine, thank you, Miss Dithermore,' he will reply, smiling like a great white shark, with the slightest giveaway trace of irritation in his voice.

Throughout this short act you, and not Miss Dithermore, will be the recipient of his full ocular attention. Once the door has closed behind

his true and trusted servant, the master invites you to help yourself.

'Sugar? cream? biscuits?'

You are free to gorge yourself. His expansive attitude creates the atmosphere of a banquet.

'Well now, let's see how you can give us a new approach.' He leans back in his chair and interlocks his fingers. Staring at the ceiling, deep in thought, he will recall the many things you have done that he has admired. 'Something on the lines of...', and he will go on to extol the virtues of adapting some of your works for their tea towels. 'We are trying to open up an entirely new range, a different concept. Something that will appeal to the husband as well as to the housewife.'

Then, if you are really unfortunate, he will be one who has to do a rough sketch of something he believes you can manage. Indeed, he might be so enthusiastic as to give you four or five ideas, all drawn in a madly advanced abstract form. When you are finally taking leave of this type, your mind, far from being creative, is spinning in an abyss of despair. Given a week or two, you may settle down to drawing up a few rough ideas. You make your appointment, with a certain number of delaying tactics on his part, and then join him at dear Miss Dithermore's coffee party.

On presentation of your roughs, he will compliment you on the designs. 'Just what I was looking for' will be the reaction. There then follows a dissertation on sales trends, the market and, most crucial of all, what happened at the board meeting.

'The board feels that, as things stand, it would, ahem, perhaps be, at this time, somewhat premature to launch whimsical tea towels.' Then, leaning forward in an almost conspiratorial fashion, as though the board had his office bugged – 'How are you on roses?'

'Whaaat!'

'We have always had a great market in rose designs. People love roses. We make a lot of money with the roses.' As he says this, he produces from under his desk a huge bundle of tea towels printed with every rose there ever was. 'We are open for this sort of thing – our ever-popular best-selling line. The board would be . . .'

The board may well have been, but I never would have. Those who cannot draw should never scribble ideas for the artist – let him do the rough talking.

The other side of the coin, the complete antithesis of the aforementioned type, are the men who know exactly what they need, and have already been assured of their directors' backing, and men like those I found in plenty in Dublin's fair city, particularly in the advertising field. You are invited down South, the date made by a casual phone call, the subject matter, with slogan, merely mentioned. You arrive at the firm's modernised offices, are ushered in to your contact, and after a welcoming swig, swept off to an upmarket restaurant. A beaming *maître d'hôtel* effuses, arms crucifixed, one extended in welcome to his honoured customer, the other indicating a reserved table. Once we are seated, he claps his hands and we are, from that moment on, attended to by what you imagine must be the entire staff. On the completion of a very rich meal indeed, several bottles of wine consumed and an indulgence in some few brandies, you are also aware of having had a most pleasant and enlightening conversation. When leaving the establishment, and after taking leave of your companion, you cannot recall ever having discussed the campaign at all. The remarkable, almost inexplicable, fact remains, you do know what you have to do. At some point during that gourmet session, the product and slogan have been mentioned, as on the phone. The rest is left to you. You are the artist they have chosen and you are given a free hand. They have studied form and reckon that they have backed the right horse.

29

FAMILY MATTERS

ART, LIKE NOSES, RUNS IN FAMILIES, so it has been said, and that would appear to be the case with the Friers family. My brothers and sisters were all adept and Mother was, I firmly believe, ahead of her time. Our offspring have been similarly endowed. Ian's son Julian is a wildlife painter of high repute and his sister Cindy, not content with shining through art college, collected young artist Chris Wilson and added him to the family circle. We had a tragic loss of talent when Ian's youngest son Quentin was killed in an accident. He had shown great promise and had been eagerly looking forward to taking up his chosen career at Bath College of Art, where he had been accepted, but sadly, fate decreed otherwise. My own sons, Jeremy and Timothy, are caught in the web. Jeremy first launched himself into culinary art and became a chef of no mean ability. After six years he lost his appetite for cooking and discarded the pan for the panchromatic. Now he happily pursues his career as a professional photographer. Timothy graduated as a graphic artist, from St Martin's College of Art in London, where he now lives and works at that particular branch of art. His real love, however, is music. He has his own band, Sun Circus, and writes and sings all his own songs. A super group, they make recordings, do gigs, and generally enjoy themselves while they await their big break.

It is a wonderful thing to be able to go through your life doing what you love and to earn money doing it. How on earth did it all start? Well, I never heard it said that my father had any leanings towards art, but I am sure, had he been so inclined, evidence would have been readily available. When I once approached my mother regarding her own abilities she, not being one, given to defeatism, claimed that she had always been very good at drawing during her schooldays. I, being a

Left to right: Yvonne, Timothy, Jeremy, myself and Vivien, with our dog, Shawcross (Photograph by Stanley Matchett)

sceptic, asked her to do a quick sketch for me, in order to detect any traces of a neglected talent. Without hesitation she drew, with great panache, the representation of something that she authoritatively claimed to be a horse. A couple of loops resembling the letter W on its side formed the mouth, and a capital M on the head effectively presented a pair of very alert ears. Both eyes sat together on one side of the head, and a sausage body carried four legs, also on the same side. A witch's broom tailed it all off. It was pure Picasso before I had even heard of that controversial artist. Perhaps she really was better than I thought at the time, but I was much too young and my critical faculties too immature to recognise genius.

Mother's artistic precociousness was to be handed down to her granddaughter when, at the tender age of nine months, my daughter Vivien introduced a new movement to an unsophisticated and disinterested world. Vivien had been bedded down for her afternoon nap, and her fond parents were awaiting the characteristic shriek that would herald her awakening. With your first-born you wait just so long; then neurosis creeps in and your imaginings become unreasonable, turning to morbid apprehensions. Vivien was a good sleeper but on this particular and memorable day Yvonne and I thought the shriek was more than a little overdue. The conviction that all was not as it should be was transmitted visually one to the other. We made for the stairway and silently and swiftly glided up to the nursery. We pressed our ears close to the door, Yvonne her left and me my right, our eyes and minds locked in fearful thought. No sounds for a longish period then, as our ears became attuned, there was the soft puffing sound of tiny feet padding around on bedclothes. Added to this, the gurgles and glugs of infantile ecstasy became audible. Our eyes met and widened in bewilderment – how could we have missed the awakening siren? Baffled, we stealthily opened the nursery door and peeped in. There she was, our clever nine-month-old, rear view on, nappy off, completely unaware of our presence, but fully absorbed in her own creativity. My mural, which decorated her little room, was in the process of being replaced by a new expressionism. She stooped down and scooped another handful from her nappy, adding a few more deft flourishes to her masterpiece. Completely oblivious of her parents, the infant phenomenon was putting her all into her own Sistine Chapel.

As years rushed past and this island cauldron bubbled with mind of bigot, gun of killer and loss of reason, my cartoon work, of necessity, changed drastically. The horrific, caustic and despairing thoughts in-filtrated and started to dominate the printed page. Senseless killings, wanton destruction, political platitudes and irreligious, sanctimonious sectarianism poisoned the pen. However ghastly the behaviour of the terrorist and however heinous the latest news headline, the resilience of our people is phenomenal and their sense of humour indestructible. Humour is man's greatest asset. It gives a sense of proportion that pre-vents our minds from totally disintegrating under stress. Out of all the carnage, the arts started to flourish. Playwrights, poets and painters drew fresh inspiration. Murals gained in popularity and gable ends started to project bold and militaristic folk art. William of Orange took second place to heraldic images, shields, red hands and mottoes in loyalist areas; portraits of Irish patriots and black-clad, heavily armed Provisionals adorned the gables in nationalist areas.

In 1978 prisoners 'on the blanket' in the Maze prison were doing something very similar to what Vivien had been doing to her nursery walls years earlier.

30
GREATNESS THRUST UPON ME

IN JUNE 1977 I WAS AWARDED an MBE for contributions to journalism and art, the journalism citation relating to newspaper cartooning. That was the Queen's jubilee year and the Northern Ireland awards were conferred at Hillsborough Castle by Her Majesty. I was not to receive my MBE from her as I was on holiday at that time, and this minor upset to Her Majesty's plans turned to my advantage. By missing Hillsborough, I was redirected to the Buckingham Palace investiture. Here the Queen Mother was to bestow the honours, her daughter being out of the country, but I cannot imagine that my failure to attend at Hillsborough influenced Her Majesty's decision to arrange a ceremonial state visit.

One sad note to the great occasion was that of all my original family only Cambridge remained to appreciate my award. She did not accompany me to London but surrendered priority to my children. What a stupendous adventure it was to go to the palace, to experience the excitement of Christopher Robin, though I was not going merely to see the changing of the guard. I had no Alice but I did have Yvonne, Vivien and Jeremy; Timothy, unfortunately, was not to enjoy the palace experience as only three members of a family are permitted to attend. It would be a very dull and unimaginative person who would feel no elation on entering that historic courtyard and joining a fashion parade equalled only by the royal enclosure at Ascot. Elegant females were dressed in multicolours for the great occasion, moving slowly around like a flowerbed caught in a gentle breeze, offset by their escorts, all uniformly clad in morning suits, just like an undertakers' convention. Expressions of joy, pride, awe, and downright disbelief were scattered generously on that sea of faces. The Horse Guards lined up on either

196

side of the entrance steps stood stiffly, like shining suits of armour. Above the gleaming breastplates and under the plumed helmets were the faces of very young men, so young that my mind's eye transformed them into a guard of honour formed by pupils of the upper sixth.

A most important-looking gentleman, the epitome of English superiority and obviously delegated to crowd control, addressed me: 'Mr Friers?'

'Yes?'

'Turn left at the top of the steps.' His long white hand fluttered like a butterfly to indicate my path.

Exhilarated by the excitement of the occasion, I had to make a joke. There are times when such an approach does not work and this was one of those times. 'Don't you want to search me?' I asked.

'Why on earth should I wish to do that?' came the ice-cold reply.

'Because I'm the only one from Northern Ireland.'

'I don't think that is at all necessary.'

An arctic winter was forecast! Whether he meant the search was unnecessary, or my attempt at levity, I did not dally to question, but took the necessary steps and turned left.

The area I entered was breathtaking, but unrelated to the speed at which I took the steps. Long and wide, with high ornate ceilings, thick carpets predominantly patterned in golds and reds, walls adorned by huge paintings, all of them old masters, it was magnificent. About one-third of the richly carpeted floor space was divided up by brass stands supporting red ropes. These served to create sub-divisions to segregate the various honours recipients. Within them stood the groups of chosen ones – men and women of all shapes and sizes. Large pompous business types chatted easily and affably amongst themselves, all giving the appearance of this being a mere commonplace. It was their club and they displayed all the assurance of having their membership fully paid up. There were fidgety people who whispered nervously and conspiratorially one to the other, sharing feelings and getting consolation out of the revelation that one was no more self-assured than the other. Then, too, you would observe the odd ones so tense and neurotic that they would have looked more appropriate in a Tower setting, awaiting the headsman's axe.

Military figures were much in evidence as they charged around in grand uniforms, some with spurs a-jangle, and white-gloved hands

197

steadying the swords at their sides. The peaks of their caps rested so far down the bridge of their noses that it seemed miraculous that they did not come to grief over one of the many obstacles which would appear on their runway. My study of the assembly and my fascination with the priceless works adorning the walls effectively dissolved my waiting time.

A disembodied and most authoritative voice boomed out my name. It echoed and re-echoed through that splendid area like the trump of Gabriel delivering the final roll call. In answer to the call I was led down a long corridor of gilded mirrors and yet more masterpieces. I could hear the guards' band playing a selection from the shows. Just then it was *Oklahoma* and I felt 'as high as an elephant's eye'. An equerry instructed me on the proper procedure before entering the grand ballroom. In a large mirror behind my tutor-in-protocol, on the crowded balcony, I could clearly discern Yvonne, Vivien and Jeremy. Yvonne, by some divine guidance, was wearing an outfit that matched to perfection the actual colours of the MBE. The three of them were seated very near the front and Jeremy, to my horror, was sitting with his back to the proceedings. This was on my mind as the equerry was saying, 'The Queen Mother may speak to you or she may not.' I had by this time forgotten about my non-appearance at Hillsborough, but sensibly dismissed the thought that such a miss would prevent the Queen Mother from speaking to me. 'She will, however, pin the order to your breast,' he interrupted my thoughts. 'You will then say, "Thank you, ma'am", bow, step backwards, and retire to the room on your right.'

On entering the grand ballroom, I kept my head rigidly directed towards the raised area where the Queen Mother was positioned, at the same time painfully screwing my eyeballs round towards the balcony to see why my son had turned his back on the proceedings. It was a relief to discover that what I had actually seen was merely his back reflected in an adjacent mirror and he, like everyone else, was taking a keen interest in the ceremony. It was a very relieved father who stood before Her Majesty.

I knew she was petite but had not imagined her to be quite as small as she was. Though she was on a raised area, it was necessary for me to bow my head slightly to meet her eyes, and what eyes she had – cornflower blue and vibrant with life. The guards were still playing 'Oh What a Beautiful Morning' – quite right too. By the Queen Mother's side stood a gigantic guardsman holding a velvet cushion upon which

198

rested the MBE. Before lifting the medal, Her Majesty started to chat. She seemed extremely well informed and asked me about cartooning. She thought it was a singularly important art form and did much to encourage rational thinking. Northern Ireland, naturally, cropped up and she said she thought it must be frightening living in such an environment. I said it was more awful being where I was at that moment, adding quickly that what I really meant was awesome. She smiled, nodded understandingly and reached for the decoration, as she assured me I was in no danger at the palace. Once she had pinned the MBE on my breast, she uttered the most perfect cue lines for an exit imaginable.

'We, as a family,' she said, 'think of you in Northern Ireland daily, and you are always in our prayers.'

'Thank you, ma'am,' I replied, bowing and stepping back. I made as good an exit as I had ever managed on a stage.

I entered the wings to discover two bored-looking gentlemen standing beside a table bearing boxes. The expression on their faces bordered on the dismal. One reached forward and 'plucked untimely' from my manly bosom the MBE for which I had apparently worked so hard. He thrust it to his fellow mournful mate, who put it in a box and snapped the lid shut at the speed of light. He then jabbed it towards me with much the same feeling that some store Santas have during the Christmas season. This bored-routine approach somewhat tarnished the glow I had been feeling. I felt like saying, 'That's no way to treat an MBE – I've a good mind to go back an' tell the Queen Morr!' But no one could really mar one's feelings on such a memorable day, nor tarnish the memory.

Four years later, on 27 June 1981, I was to receive an honorary MA from the Open University, an honour of which I am extremely proud and for which I will be eternally grateful.

31
WHATSITSNAME

'WOULD YOU RATHER BE remembered as an artist or a cartoonist?' – now there is a question often directed at me. It makes me wonder, is a cartoonist not an artist? Were Honoré Daumier and Gustave Doré not artists, and was there not more fuss made over the possible sale out of England of a cartoon by Leonardo than there was over the temporary loss of his *Mona Lisa*? Why do people always think of cartoons as funny drawings or topical commentaries in newspapers? A cartoon is a black and white drawing, it may be humorous or it could be the initial design for a stained-glass window. Most, if not all, of the greatest artists have drawn cartoons; not all, however, have been lampoonists, which is the art form really referred to in the question. Lampooning is the art of satirising, criticising, or even ridiculing, in drawing or in prose. The average person conceives of the cartoon as a funny drawing, which is not entirely correct. Many there are who dismiss these drawings with a short chuckle and never consider them as serious contributions to the world of art. Without doubt there are very many lampoons that are merely quips, and all too many are shorthand scrawls, but the Gilrays, Hogarths, Thelwells, Illingworths, Searles, Scarfes and Steadmans of this world can never be dismissed lightly as contenders for a place among the serious contributors to our artistic heritage.

'Would you rather be remembered as an artist or a cartoonist?' The answer is, 'as both' – but to be remembered affectionately is what most people desire.

I was sitting in the bar of the Ulster Arts Club on Elmwood Avenue one evening chatting with the late John D. Stewart when the conversation

"Derry ? – Why you can't even see IRELAND !"

turned to my name, its pronunciation and its origin. Quite naturally the subject of cartoons arose too and my name, so closely linked with that art form, seemed to have become an obsession with John D.

'Do you know what "Rowel" means?' he asked me.

'Of course I do,' I replied, feeling somewhat affronted that he should think I would not know the origin and meaning of my own name. I told him Rowel, my Christian name, was taken from a great-grandmother whose maiden name was Harriet Rowell. The second 'l' was dropped and my name became Rowel. This spelling, I told him, was, according to the dictionary derivation, 'a small wheel with radiating points, forming the extremity of a horseman's spur'.

'Exactly,' said John D 'Why don't you use it in conjunction with your signature?'

'I had thought of it, but just didn't bother,' was my nonchalant reply. Being the intense person that he was, John D. was nonplussed by my statement.

'But Rowel, it's a natural symbol, a veritable gift for a cartoonist. You must use it. You are a deflator of pomposity, an artist who laughs and pokes fun at the foibles of fools and your rapier is thrust at the evil and narrow minds which surround us,' he pronounced, with such serious intensity that it made a deep and instant impression on me.

Shortly after said conversation with John D., but a long time after *Dublin Opinion*, I started to add the spur to my signature on cartoons.

That is how the 'wee star', as some people call it, became a part of my signature. There are those who wonder why I do not include it on paintings, but it is singularly inappropriate to that aspect of my work.

People's names are my Achilles heel. For them, I have the memory of a goldfish. It is said that if a goldfish passes one of those ornamental rock sculptures which decorate their bowls or tanks, when they repass a few seconds later they do not remember that they have seen it before. I wonder how anyone can read the mind of a goldfish to acquire such useful knowledge. Fish talk to themselves. We can see them do that as they mooch around behind the glass. If it is true that their memories are that bad, then where names are concerned – I'm a goldfish.

My strong defence against accusations of senility, snootiness or downright stupidity, is that in my professional life I meet so many thousands of people who already know me, or think they know me, through familiarity with my work, or seeing me on television, or hearing me on radio. I have given talks to thousands, and after each and every address, that cup of tea and buns can put the majority on Christian name terms with me. The faces, as you would expect, register strongly, but that plethora of names which assails the brain is transformed into a well-shuffled pack of cards. Many times, as I have walked along a street with Yvonne, a friendly face looms up, beaming delighted familiarity. Yvonne, naturally, asks me who that nice person is. Through the side of my mouth, cunningly concealed in what is meant to be a smile, I inform her that I do not have a clue. Then, still with the twisted smile, I tell her that she must pretend I was just talking about them, so that I simply have to say, 'Hello, lovely to meet you again. You haven't met my wife Yvonne, have you?' That solves great embarrassment, provided that in the panic I can still remember my wife's name.

The cartooning side of the art world has its obvious advantages as a reputation builder – constant media appearances guarantee that. With the political cartoon, you meet and come to know many politicians, and even more of them know you. With each new Northern Ireland secretary of state a dinner party is organised so that he will get to know people, and who better to be friendly with than the cartoonist? Such forethought could be an insurance policy, although obviously not comprehensive. The 'whatsitsname syndrome' lives and thrives on these occasions, and it was at one such event that I was saved embarrassment by a quip. Humphrey Atkins had a dinner party at Hillsborough. Twelve

BLANKETY BLANK

"I asked them for a political solution and the answer was — BLANK!"

couples were seated at the table, and it was all very pleasant. The food was good and the wine and conversation flowed most convivially. The moment arrived when the ladies retired to adjust their faces and the men were left to finish their port and cigars, to make or mar their reputations through the quality of their stories. When the ladies had completed their cosmetic refreshments and the husbands had been summoned to join them, I was first off the mark. Mrs Atkins stood at the entrance to the large and imposing drawing room filled with wives and an accompanying babble of animated conversation. As I was about to enter, Mrs Atkins whispered something to me which instantly set my alarm bells ringing. A nasty fit of the premonitions grabbed hold of me – I knew what would follow, and it did.

'Rowel' – she got my name right – 'you know what our life style is like, one meets so many people . . .'

I looked desperately round the assembled wives and not only was I unable to think of one name, but my panic also blurred their faces. The cartoonist in me came to the rescue. With what I should hope was a twinkle in my eye, I said, 'I know exactly what you mean. What did you say your name was?' She not only enjoyed the joke, but instantly knew she had a soul mate. I had saved face.

32

THE MAN WHO LOVED PAISLEY,
AND A CASE OF MISTAKEN IDENTITY

O N THE WAY TO A MEETING OF THE executive of the Cystic Fibrosis Trust, of which I am Northern Ireland chairman, I stood surrounded by vacant-eyed troglodytes in London's Piccadilly Circus tube station. As that familiar rush of warm air which heralds an approaching train stood my hair on end, a large figure loomed out of the 'vacant lot' and headed straight towards me. He was around six feet four inches tall and in his late thirties. He wore a large bright red sweater, a large bright grin and his chin was adorned with designer stubble. 'How's about ye, man,' he roared in a broad Scottish accent, as he wrapped one huge arm around my shoulders. A clean and respectable-looking Bohemian, he was not one of that underground world's usual dropouts. The only smell from his person was overpowering and very much over-the-limit alcoholic. It was as though he had known me for years, and I was strangely unperturbed by his familiarity.

'Where do ye come frae?' he asked.

'Northern Ireland,' I replied.

'Good fur yew!' he roared, hugging me with unbridled delight. I must admit to a certain feeling of misgiving at this emphatic demonstration of his bonhomie. Happily, it was only momentary. With one arm around my shoulder, he extended the other and, opening a large clenched fist, he revealed a mouth organ.

'Ah foun' this in a bin; Ah wuz lookin' fur somethin' tae eat,' he said.

I found it hard to imagine that at any time this character could have been searching in bins for food. Nothing about him suggested hard times, and under-nourishment could have been no more to him than another big word.

'Ah canna play the bloody thing,' said he, 'but Ah'll try.'

The train arrived and the squeeze was on. Protected by my newly acquired friendly giant, I had no trouble boarding. As the tube doors closed, he had his shot at playing the harmonica. A few of the dead faces on the train actually expressed consciousness. Their pain was all too evident. A man of obvious sensitivity, he removed the so-called musical instrument from his mouth and stuck it in his pocket.

'Ach, Ah canna play the bloody thing,' he pronounced, as though it were a startling discovery. 'So ye come frae Northern Ireland?'

'Yes,' I replied, as my ears popped back to normality.

'Do ye know the Big Man?'

The question had me stumped. 'The Big Man?' I asked, no doubt looking every bit as vague as I felt.

'Aye, the Big Man – ye know, the Big Man,' said he, with emphasis and obvious surprise at my apparent ignorance.

I looked at him vacantly and played about with the description, transposing it into the Big Yin, and automatically Billy Connolly leaped to mind. This notion was dashed from my thoughts by the intrusion of his loud voice.

'Dr Paisley,' he roared. 'Dr Paisley, he called the pope the anti-christ – good for him! He called him the anti-christ at the EEC. Do ye know him?' he asked, looking keenly down into my eyes.

I told him I did.

'Ya do nawt,' said he.

'I do,' said I.

'Personally?'

It was virtually a plea. He needed the answer I gave him.

'Yes.'

His eyes lit up with obvious delight. He thrust a huge hand out and squeezed mine until the metacarpals almost ignited as they rubbed together.

'Ah love that man,' he roared, 'Ah love him.'

The train stopped at Leicester Square.

'Ah haf tae get aff here,' he said as he dived out onto the platform.

As the doors slowly hissed shut, the huge Scot stood with his hands cupped and roared in at me.

'Tell the Big Man Ah love him.' The voice boomed out above the sounds of people stampeding in before the doors closed. It bounced all around the carriage and almost wakened dead commuters. For the first time I felt uncomfortable. I imagined that power of love echoing along the Tubes – Piccadilly line, Metropolitan, Circle, all along the network, coming up at Marble Arch, the Temple, Tooting Broadway, Hatton Cross and everywhere throughout that system. 'Ah love him, Ah love him,' bursting forth at all stations like the Hallelujah Chorus.

I was sitting at Heathrow the next day, waiting to board the plane for Belfast and home, when, looking up from where I was at the bar end of the area, I saw the Big Man himself enter at the other end with his two bodyguards. Once on board the plane, I was seated about five rows from the front. Dr Paisley and company were last to board and sat in the front seats. After food and drinks were served, nature prompted me to make use of the forward convenience. As I passed the good doctor he looked up and said to me, 'Congratulations on Brazil.' To say I was slightly baffled by his comment would not be incorrect. I was totally bewildered. In the littlest room I pondered. What could I have done in Brazil to deserve congratulations, and how did Dr Paisley know something about me of which I myself was completely ignorant?

As I exited from my comfort station I looked towards the Big Man. He was smiling the broadest of smiles and slowly wagging his head. When I stepped in his direction, he put up his hand to stay me.

'I must apologise, Rowel, for what I just said a moment ago.'

'Oh yes?'

'You realise, of course,' he continued, 'that Heathrow waiting area is a very large area and you were away at one end and I was at the other. As I looked away up to where you were, I turned to my two friends here and I said "There's Harry Cavan".'

I did not know how to take the remark, but my conceit prevailed. There is a superficial similarity between the soccer supremo and myself, but I think I win by a nose.

'Now, the reason I mentioned Brazil,' said the good doctor, 'is because Harry Cavan has a sister who is in the mission field in Brazil and is doing excellent work. Excellent work.'

Having had everything clarified, I was about to embark on the Scotsman and his love when the hostess intervened, informing me that we were about to land and asking me to belt up.

33

TROUBLES

TO LIVE IN IRELAND IS TO LIVE on a volcanic island; it has always been, may always be, a land of turbulence. Long before my entry into the world in 1920, to this tragic drama which is our unfortunate birthright, our small island has been dogged by constant eruptions, when the molten lava of religious and political hatred bursts forth, leaving trails of terror and destruction in its wake. In Northern Ireland, all is borne with a stoicism and a courage that equates with, even excels, that which earned Malta a George Cross in the Second World War.

Since my childhood, when I beat a tin can like the rest of my pals in our Protestant area of east Belfast and sang of the sash that my father never wore but my great-grandfather did, I have lived through the sickness which is Ireland's, without ever wishing to leave her shores.

When I was working in Allen's during the thirties I used to hear the stutter of machine-gun fire and outside the doors used to see police tenders speed along Corporation Street. I remember the controversial B Specials patrolling the streets and I later immortalised them in a series of cartoons for Queen's University's rag magazine, *Pro Tanto Quid*. Throughout my young life the outbursts were sporadic, and although serious enough, offered no great threat to commerce, being, as they were, contained by the Royal Ulster Constabulary and the B Specials. My cartoons in those early days were seldom comments on political events, and politicians were immune. Had I, at that time, been a commentator on the political scene, I feel sure it would not have been easy to get into print. I recall on one occasion suggesting a cartoon to the then editor of the *Belfast Telegraph*, Jack Sayers, on a topic that necessitated the inclusion of the education minister for Northern Ireland, Harry Midgley, but

I was gently reprimanded for having such an idea. 'We couldn't poke fun at Harry,' he said, smiling. There were times when an idea would be begging for print, yet it would not be 'quite the thing to do'. To me then, and now, the idea that you did not criticise your friends was provincialism at its worst.

My first essay into the forbidden territory occurred in 1962, when the Reverend Ian Paisley hit the headlines with his denunciation of ecumenicism. The newspaper billboards announced, 'Paisley for Rome'. Driving from Dublin with my photographer friend Leslie Stuart, I commented on these billboards and remarked that I could see the writing on the wall. From this trip was born a cartoon set in Rome, with St Peter's in the background, and in the middle distance two *carabinieri*, and an urchin scribbling graffiti on the walls of the Café de Roma – 'No Paisley here'. Jack Sayers liked that one and it was published. He would have liked me to mount a full-frontal attack on the reverend gentleman at that time, but my instincts and some anonymous letters convinced me that it was too soon and would have savoured somewhat of a personal vendetta.

It was not until quite a few moons later that another bolt was fired at that target area. This cartoon sprang from the incarceration of Mr Paisley and another reverend colleague. The billboards bluntly announced that they were 'jailed'. It was the summer of 1969, with splendid weather. I drew a beach scene with two fat ladies sunbathing, and beside them slept a man with a newspaper over his head to protect him from the sun (and to give the artist an excuse to display the news headline).

208

The first book published by Blackstaff Press was *Riotous Living* in 1971; here I am signing Erskine Mayne's window in Donegall Square West. (Courtesy of *Belfast Telegraph*)

One lady is remarking to the other, 'Isn't it a shame to be stuck inside in lovely weather like this?' In 1969 the battle of Burntollet, with its batons and boots, changed my direction as a cartoonist. Now I was faced with having to take an interest in the political scene and its accompanying mayhem.

As I write, more than twenty-five years on, the scene scarcely seems to have changed. Thousands have been murdered, politicians are still agreeing to disagree, security is sneered at, and the bombers and gunmen remain unyielding in their bid to destroy the country they claim to love. The newspaper cartoonist's main topic is now dictated by the bomb and the gun. Symbolic figures representing death and destruction replace the funny characters. Indiscriminate bombings of public places such as hotels and bars took, and still take, their deadly toll. The machine gun cut down worshippers in church and fire bombs gutted the La Mon House Hotel, claiming twelve blameless lives in an inferno of death where people had been enjoying their annual get-together. Train and bus stations, shops and even private houses came under attack. Innocent people were cut down by terrorist guns, Catholic and Protestant alike. Nothing was sacrosanct. A bomb at Enniskillen's War Memorial on Remembrance Day, 1987, became only one of countless atrocities to shock the world.

The politicians, naturally enough, now became major ingredients for the cartoonist. As the battle raged round them, they engaged in their own war of words and made their own disagreements. The church leaders piously expressed disapproval but made no impression on a cynical and godless society. Secretaries of state have come and gone, each making his own mark (though little impression) on the scene. Attitudes remain as stubborn as always and there are so many bends in the tunnel that it is hard to know if the light exists.

Of all the Northern Ireland secretaries of state, Merlyn Rees was my favourite, not as a model for caricature – Willie Whitelaw won that hands down – but as a person easy to talk to and who listened to what you had to say. He owns a cartoon of mine, a Wild West scene depicting a bunch of Northern Ireland politicians riding into town – and obviously not on a peace mission. Sheriff Ted Heath lounges on a chair outside the sheriff's office with his deputy Francis Pym saying, 'Man, we got problems!' Now, before this cartoon was submitted for printing by the press, a general election ran that particular sheriff out of town. I performed a major transplant operation, replacing Heath with Harold Wilson, and Pym with Merlyn Rees. Years later, when I was chatting one day to Gerry Fitt at Westminster, Merlyn Rees appeared on the

'Man, we got problems!'

scene. He reminded me of the cartoon and, said he, 'There was a great deal more behind it than anyone realised.'

I remember meeting Rees's wife Colleen at a Royal Ulster Academy of Arts exhibition. She took me by the arm saying, 'I've seen one of your pictures. Will you show me the other?' As we walked down the gallery she asked me what I thought of her husband, not politically, but from the caricaturist's point of view. This I did without pulling any punches. She looked at me, laughed, and remarked that she really would have to tidy him up. Hastily, I warned her against any such drastic action as it might leave nothing at all for the caricaturist.

The Reverend Joseph Parker, whose son Stephen, aged fourteen, was killed when trying to warn of a bomb on Bloody Friday, 21 July 1972, approached me in March 1974 to help him with his peace bid. Nine people had been killed and one hundred and thirty injured by the nineteen Provisional IRA bombs planted that Friday. Joseph Parker, a kind and gentle man, was devastated by the death of his son and deeply disturbed by the whole situation. He wanted me to do some posters to display outside the Belfast City Hall. They were of biblical quotations such as 'I was a stranger and ye took me in', which depicted a hooded

211

figure with hands tied behind his back and blood pouring from the hood. 'The same yesterday –' showed death with his sickle dripping blood, and the dates 1690, 1798, 1916, and 1969. Ten such posters were displayed; they created an impression but unfortunately only of short duration – so often the case in hell's island.

Of the many melancholy and deeply depressing incidents I have been impelled to comment on, few have left such a shadow on my mind as the death of Bobby Sands...

The Europa Hotel was packed with pressmen from all parts of the globe. Like hungry vultures they had waited while Bobby Sands's hunger strike had drawn to its inevitable end. My telephone rang and an American voice introduced the caller as a television production man. He had been directed to me by the BBC who had told him I was fast at visuals. 'We would like you to go up to Bobby Sands's house,' he said. 'People are viewing the body and we would like you to do so on our behalf. No photographers are allowed so we would like you to do an artist's impression for us.'

I must admit this request sent an involuntary shudder through me. It was not the sort of commission to relish. The first thought that came to me was: is this not an invasion of privacy? That, to anyone with feelings, would be the natural reaction, but in this world we live in, sensitivity is eclipsed by the media's hunger. Family feelings take second place to the organisation. I had grave misgivings about taking the commission, so much so that I phoned my friend and one-time northern editor of the *Irish Times*, Conor O'Clery.

I explained my predicament and said, 'If you were me, would you do it?'

Always the professional newspaper man, he said: 'If I were you, I probably wouldn't, but if I were myself, I most certainly would.'

I thanked him for his words and decided that, as I was also a newspaper man, I had better be professional and do what was expected of me. I accepted and a car was sent to take me to Twinbrook in west Belfast.

Everything was still and the only sound was the gentle crunch of the car tyres on the tarmac. The gable ends of the houses displayed posters bearing photographic likenesses of the hunger strikers. Black flags hung limp and motionless from the windows of the estate. The presence of death could never have been more evident. As my car glided to a stop,

212

I saw the long queue across the road move slowly and silently towards the open door of the Sands home. A man at the door directed people in and out of the small house. Those coming out had their heads bowed, the occasional index finger or handkerchief brushing a cheek. They moved off, conversing among themselves in low whispers.

The long queue of sympathisers was still growing as I took my place in the line. As I stood there in that atmosphere of grim finality, in my thoughts I conjured up the young, handsome, smiling face of Bobby Sands that had appeared almost daily in the newspapers and on television. I was still holding the picture of his youthful freshness in my mind, and wondering how long this nightmare of ours was to last, when the man at the door roused me with, 'Go on in now and be quick; there's a lot of people still to come.'

The coffin sat close to the wall on two trestles. It was two-thirds covered by a tricolour on which rested black gloves and a beret. At attention, black-uniformed, with dark glasses and fully armed, two men stood forming a guard of honour at each end of the coffin. A heap of mass cards lay on the flag. Rosary beads, entwined in the skeletal hands, lay stark against the cards, the crucifix predominant. The head on the pillow paralysed me, and mixed emotions of horror and deep pity swept through me. This was the face of an old man – more than that, it was the face of death itself. What I saw bore no resemblance to Bobby Sands, and the image of death I witnessed then will live with me for ever. Anyone who saw him as I did will never forget Bobby Sands because they will know how hellish the suffering he had endured must have been.

When I got back to the Europa the television director asked for three drawings, a general one, a close-up of the face, and another of the hands and beads. It was not a difficult assignment to carry out from memory, for that image can never be erased. Once I had completed the required drawings, I was to return and make a sketch in the church where the body rested. Not more than twenty minutes after the completion of those drawings, they were, through the wonder of satellites, being viewed in the United States. That was one of the most harrowing, and at the same time most awesome, experiences in all my professional career. It was a chapter of history which had to be recorded and it was my lot to make that recording.

34

TALE END

MY COUSIN REGGIE MILLAR HAD as a very young man emigrated to the Americas. Now retired, he lives in Huntington Beach, California. When he came over here in the summer of 1992 I saw him again after half a century of non-communication. With his three brothers and one sister, I was delighted to join in a memorable family reunion. Out of this gathering of the clans, an invitation to visit him and his offspring at home in California was offered so warmly that it could not be refused. Thus it was that Yvonne and I went to spend three weeks in sunny California, in the autumn of 1992.

Reggie and his daughter Marilyn could not have made us more welcome. They did everything to make that holiday special and in this department they passed with flying colours. Reggie, who loves driving and seems a natural tour guide, took us everywhere. We went to Las Vegas, the Grand Canyon, Hollywood and Universal Studios, San Francisco, Malibu, San Diego and Long Island. We visited Steinbeck's Monterey, Clint Eastwood's pub, the Hog's Breath, in Carmel, and the golf course at Pebble Beach. We drank orange juice squeezed from the fruit which grew on the trees in my cousin's garden in Orange County and I downed tequila in the approved manner, with salt and lime, in Rosarito, Mexico. The holiday was in late October, taking in Hallowe'en and the preparations for Thanksgiving. These two events seemed, in my cousin's priorities, anyway, to be more important than the struggle for presidential power between Bill Clinton and George Bush. Where the first man and lady of America were concerned in that household, Rowel and Yvonne had already been elected.

From the constant blue skies of California and a temperature in the eighties, we returned to the grey skies and bare trees of an Irish winter.

It was now 26 January 1993. Gale force winds had been shrieking around the house, rattling the windows like some demented spirit seeking sanctuary. Young trees snapped in the fierce gusts and the old ones, which had resisted such elemental outbursts for too many years, crashed to earth. The ferries were curtailed and television's weathermen, in the studio's warmth, calmly and smilingly tried to make it all sound matter-of-fact as they played with their little black clouds and arrows on the meteorological maps.

I stood looking out of my studio window. The rain drifted down like a muslin veil, creating a multi-grey world. Sheets of rain ran gently down my studio's roof lights and in the garden skeletal trees, wet and sombre, waved slowly and silently, as if mourning the sun's demise. The studio, now mainly used by my son Jeremy for his photography, looks down on the garden about forty feet below. As I looked down at the twisting paths, the steps and the fish ponds, I thought of how long it had taken us to make our impression on what had once been nothing more than a field with a couple of trees in it. Three designers had worked for years on it – Yvonne, Jeremy and myself. My eyes, penetrating the rain veil, wandered dreamily over the mini-landscape of shrubs and trees, each in its own pastel shade of grey. Raising my gaze slightly above the surrounding garden wall, I caught a glimpse of yellow light coming from a window. The white cottages of Brook Street, one-time homes of mill workers, stood out in the mistiness to create a phantom image, an image of childhood and the Lagan Village, a nostalgic reminder of my past, right beside me, and never before had I been aware of the similarity.

I turned from the window and moved towards my drawing table, an item of furniture I only use when doing very large drawings. I sat on the stool, and leaning on the table with my chin cupped in my hands, I looked through the rain-crazed glass of the roof lights at the un-compromising slate-coloured canopy overhead. Further outlook was positively unsettled. People were still being shot and political vision was as shrouded as the weather. Funerals, accusations, demands for inquiries, random shootings, terrorist bomb blasts and political bombast – nothing was improving. Deepest despondency was setting in fast and I could do little to prevent it.

From one dark corner of the studio I sensed a presence and my eyes wandered in that direction. That presence suddenly became the most important thing in the studio. It was the tall Victorian easel of William

215

Conor – the easel he had bequeathed to me. As I became conscious of it, my morose thoughts vanished and I recalled the last large drawing I had had on my drawing table. It was a five-foot-by-three-foot portrait group of Colin Middleton, John Luke, Padraic Woods, Maurice Wilks, Frank McKelvey and William Conor, entitled *The Old Masters*. It is now in the Ulster Museum's permanent collection along with a companion piece portraying Basil Blackshaw, Neil Shawcross, David Evans, John Turner, Tom Carr and Raymond Piper. That easel brought me back to a more optimistic frame of mind. I began to think how lucky I was to be born with a gift, a gift which gives me and gives others pleasure, which I can use happily to earn my living and which at the same time offers me the rare opportunity of meeting and making friends with so many people.

On Saturday 29 May 1993, at the Royal Ulster Academy of Arts' annual general assembly, I was handed the president's chain of office – thirty-six years after William Conor's election to that office, when I was his vice-president. Conor's easel, like Aladdin's lamp, had its own magic and it had it in plenty on that occasion. It made me realise how fortunate I was in my family and in my friends, many famous, others not so famous, but not one more important than the other. To them all, living and dead, I dedicate my story.

The Old Masters
Left to right: Colin Middleton, John Luke, William Conor, Padraic Woods, Maurice Wilks and Frank McKelvey (Courtesy of the Board of Trustees of the Ulster Museum)